Castles and Fortifications of BRITAIN and IRELAND

By the same author

Neolithic Cultures of North Africa
History from the Earth
Prehistoric Britain and Ireland
Hillforts of the Iron Age in England and Wales
Hadrian's Wall

J. Forde-Johnston

Castles and Fortifications of
BRITAIN
and
IRELAND

J. M. Dent & Sons Ltd

London, Toronto & Melbourne

First published 1977
© J. Forde-Johnston 1977

Made in Great Britain by
Butler & Tanner Ltd,
Frome and London

for
J. M. DENT & SONS LTD
Aldine House, Albemarle Street, London

This book is set in Monophoto Baskerville 11 pt

ISBN 0 460 04195 9

British Library Cataloguing in Publication Data

Forde-Johnston, James
    Castles and fortifications of Britain and Ireland.
    1. Fortification – Great Britain
    I. Title
    623'.1'0941   UG429.G7
    ISBN 0 460 04195 9

Contents

Acknowledgments

The author wishes to thank the following for permission to use their photographs: Cambridge University Collection—copyright reserved (Plates 3, 4, 5, 6, 7, 16, 17, 20, 21, 24); Bord Fáilte Photo (Plates 9, 10, 11, 33, 89, 91); Crown copyright—reproduced with the permission of the Controller of Her Majesty's Stationery Office (Plates 12, 97, 98, 99, 100, 103, 104, 105); the British Tourist Authority (Plates 23, 28, 31, 54, 55, 58, 60, 62); National Monuments Record (Plates 25, 36, 38); Northern Ireland Tourist Board (Plates 37, 96); Commissioners of Public Works in Ireland (Plates 41, 85, 86, 87, 88, 90, 92, 93, 94, 95); Scottish Tourist Board (Plates 42, 45, 78, 79, 81, 82, 83, 84); Wales Tourist Board (Plates 57, 64); William Heinemann Ltd (Figs 17, 18, 19, 22, 23, 24, 25); Stewart Cruden and Thomas Nelson & Sons Ltd (Fig. 26); Dundalgan Press Ltd, Dundalk (Fig. 28).

List of Line Drawings

List of Plates

Introduction

Apart from the very recent past, man's building efforts have been concentrated on a very few main types of structure: houses, tombs, temples and, inevitably it seems, fortifications. Defensive works seem to have occupied a prominent place at all periods and in all areas. They appear in the very early stages of urban life, protecting Jericho *c.* 7000 BC, and they appear in all areas, from Finland to Fiji and from Athens to the Andes. There are very few parts of the world in which fortifications are not recorded in some period of history. Some, such as the great medieval castles, are very familiar to us; others, such as Maori or Fijian earthworks or the great fortresses of South America, less so.

The same variation obtains in the British Isles which, although it cannot claim the full span of *c.* 9000 years mentioned above, nevertheless participates fully in the story of fortification, with a history stretching over two and a half thousand years, embracing such varied structures as Iron Age forts, Scottish brochs, Roman legionary fortresses, Anglo-Saxon *burhs*, Norman castles, medieval town walls, Irish tower-houses and many more. Although exact numbers are hard to come by, there must be remains of more than ten thousand fortifications, of all types, still visible in the British Isles, even if not all of them are as prominent and as

easy to find as the castles at Dover, Conway, Bamburgh or Carrickfergus.

The purpose of this book is to draw attention to the range of structures which served the different periods as far as defence was concerned, with particular reference to surviving remains, not to write a history of fortification in the British Isles, which is a technical matter. Hopefully it will increase the understanding and appreciation of the rich heritage of structural remains which still survive in these islands, for the pleasure and instruction of those who care to go and seek them out for themselves. The only real answer to all the threats to our ancient monuments is an informed general public, and it is the writer's hope that this book will provide some small help in that direction.

J. Forde-Johnston
Manchester 1977

1 Prehistoric Fortification

Although there is some evidence from the Upper Palaeolithic period (*c.* 40,000–10,000 BC), building as a major human preoccupation began in the ancient Near East just after 10,000 BC, following the discovery of plant cultivation and livestock breeding. Control of his food supply enabled man to develop a more settled pattern of life, in permanent houses and settlements, in contrast to his former nomadic existence. In the 3000 years between *c.* 9000 and 6000 BC there was a considerable development of agricultural villages in the Near East and, significantly for the purpose of this book, the first evidence of fortification, at the ancient site of Jericho, possibly as early as 7000 BC. The evidence consists of a massive stone wall and a ditch, apparently surrounding the settlement, and a circular tower, presumably a watch-tower. Thus the earliest fortification known is a town wall, and the town or city wall was to remain one of the most widespread types of fortification throughout history. Inevitably, in time, more specialized forms developed, such as the purpose-built Roman fort or medieval castle, but the enclosing, protective wall around settlement or city always remained a fundamental type, and provides an appropriate starting point for the first topic to be dealt with, prehistoric fortification. There are, in fact, three main types of structure in the British Isles to be dealt with under this heading: hillforts, duns and brochs. Hillforts are found in all four countries (England, Ireland, Scotland and Wales), while duns and brochs are confined to Scotland, although there are one or two stone structures in Ireland which need to be noted in the same context.

Hillforts

Over much of southern and western England, most of Wales, the lowlands of Scotland and many parts of Ireland, grass-grown banks and ditches (Pl. 1) or tumbled masses of loose stones, encircling hilltops and cutting off promontories, form the still substantial remains of some 3000 prehistoric fortifications built during the last seven or eight centuries before the Roman Conquest (*c.* 800 BC–AD 43). The general term used for all of these structures is *hillforts*, although not all of them are on hills. The term *defensive enclosures*, however, makes a better starting point for descriptive purposes. They are essentially areas of open ground surrounded by, or in the case of promontories cut off by, a wall or walls, supplemented in many cases by ditches, in much the same way as a town wall surrounded the area of a town. Hillforts were not buildings in the sense of having four walls and a roof. Even the smallest

1 Mam Tor, Derbyshire.

sites, an acre or less in area, were much
too big for that. Any roofed structures
they did contain were simply huts or
houses belonging to the settlements which
existed within some, but by no means all
of them, for hillforts appear to have had
functions apart from habitation. In their
size (over 200 acres in some cases), and
their numbers (over 3000), they form the
most substantial monumental remnant of
the prehistoric period, and even today
their visible remains are eloquent
testimony to the building capabilities of
the early inhabitants of the British Isles.

In spite of their numbers hillforts in the
British Isles are only part of a much larger
picture embracing many parts of central
and western Europe. European hillforts
first appear in the Late Bronze Age period
(*c.* 1200–800 BC), in the north Alpine

region (south-west Germany, south-east
France and northern Switzerland),
possibly as a result of ideas from the
Mycenaean world in Greece, possibly even
as a result of the collapse of Mycenae
itself, *c.* 1100 BC. From the north Alpine
region there was a progressive expansion
of population, most particularly in the
(now iron-using) periods known as
Hallstatt (700–500 BC) and La Tène (500
BC onwards), which carried the idea of
hillforts to many parts of Europe,
including the British Isles. In the British
Isles hillforts have traditionally been
attributed to the Iron Age period, and
indeed to the latter part of it, from *c.* 350
BC on, implying that the idea of
fortification took some 700 years to reach
here from the north Alpine area. It is
quite clear, however, that in their origins

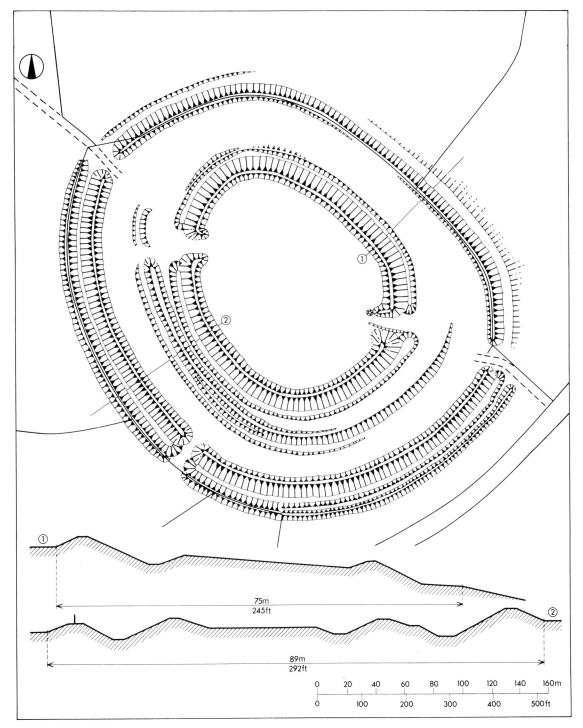

Fig. 1 Warbstow Bury, Cornwall.

at least hillforts are Late Bronze Age rather than Iron Age, so that the term Iron Age hillfort so long attached to them here may no longer be appropriate. There is a growing acceptance of the idea that, in the British Isles as in Europe, hillforts began in the Late Bronze Age and lasted throughout the Iron Age, occupying, as already indicated, the last seven or eight centuries before the Roman Conquest.

Of the 3000 or so hillforts in the British Isles about 1500 are found in England and Wales, mostly in the triangular area formed by the south and west coasts and a line from the Mersey to the mouth of the Thames. There is a somewhat smaller number in Scotland (*c.* 1000), with the main concentration in the counties immediately beyond the English border. The 500 or so forts allowed for Ireland represent guesswork rather than established fact. There are many thousands of defensive enclosures there, belonging to all periods, but which are prehistoric and which later it is difficult to say.

Although not all hillforts are situated on hills, most of them nevertheless take some advantage of natural features—hilltops, promontories, ridges, cliff edges—the objective being to secure sloping ground below some if not all of the man-made defences. In a small number of cases the natural feature is a lake or river, the ground being otherwise flat, and in other cases again there are no natural features whatsoever, the ground around the site being entirely flat. The majority of hillforts fall into one of two major classes as far as situation is concerned: they are either contour forts or promontory forts. In broad terms a contour fort is one which is situated on a hilltop, its defences being deemed to follow the contours of the hill, hence the name. A promontory fort has natural defences on two or three sides and man-made defences only on the remainder of the perimeter, obviously a great economy in building effort. In other situations a section of ridge is cut off by

two ramparts, or a section of a cliff edge by a U-shaped rampart, but these and other situations indicated above are very much in a minority as compared with the two major categories.

Some indication of the upper end of the size range has been given already. In fact, only three sites (Bindon, Dorset; Ham Hill, Somerset; Hengistbury Head, Hants) are of the size mentioned (over 200 acres), and there is only a handful of sites over 50 acres in area. The majority of hillforts fall into two size categories and it is noticeable that the two tend to occupy different areas, although the pattern is not absolute and there is some overlap. Something like three-quarters of all hillforts (i.e. *c.* 2200 sites) are 3 acres or less in area, some of them very much less. These small sites are found mainly in western and northern regions, that is, south-west England, Wales, Scotland and Ireland. Most of the remaining sites are between 3 and 30 acres in area, and these occur in southern and south-eastern England, the Cotswolds and the Welsh border counties, particularly Herefordshire and Shropshire.

Whatever their size or situation, all hillforts belong to one of three types according to their defences: univallate forts, multivallate forts, and multiple-enclosure forts. A univallate fort (Latin *vallum*, rampart) is one which is defended by a single rampart, usually, but not always, accompanied by a frontal ditch (Pl. 1). A multivallate fort has two or more ramparts, accompanied again more often than not by ditches (Pl. 2). In both of these groups the defences surround a single enclosure. Sites in the third group (multiple-enclosure forts) consist of two or more enclosures, side by side or concentric, or a combination of the two, linked together by defences which can be either univallate or multivallate or a mixture of the two. About two-thirds of all hillforts are of the relatively simple univallate type (i.e. *c.* 2000 sites). The bulk of the remainder are multivallate, with a smaller number of multiple-enclosure sites.

2 Old Oswestry, Shropshire.

Excavation in some 300 sites has produced a considerable body of evidence on the original structure and appearance of hillforts. The main structural features involved are ramparts, ditches, berms and counterscarp banks and these, in various combinations, provide what may be termed the defence systems of hillforts. Ramparts are of two main types, *glacis* (pronounced glassy) and revetted. Glacis or sloping-fronted ramparts are triangular in cross-section with a continuous slope, *c*. 35–40 degrees, from the bottom of the accompanying ditch (which this type must have to make it effective) to the rampart crest, and it is this slope or glacis (from a French military engineering term) which is deemed to provide the main obstacle to an attacker. Most glacis ramparts consist of a simple dump of material from the ditch (Fig. 2, a) but in one or two larger examples there is elaborate stonework at the back acting as a buttress (Fig. 2, g).

The alternative to the glacis or sloping-fronted rampart is the revetted type in which a vertical rather than a sloping front is presented to the enemy. The revetment can be either stone or timber, and the rear of the rampart can be finished off in various ways, by a sloping ramp, by a series of steps or by a second,

back revetment, giving the rampart a box-like cross-section, hence the term box-rampart. The internal structure of revetted ramparts shows some variation, but they all have in common a vertical front, topped by a breastwork, as the main defensive feature (Fig. 2, c–f). In a small number of cases there are hybrid ramparts combining a glacis slope with a vertical revetment at the top (Fig. 2,b).

The second main defence feature is the outer ditch. As well as providing the material for the rampart, this is, in many cases, a very considerable obstacle in its own right. With the exception of rock-cut ditches, which tend to be somewhat irregular, most ditches are V-shaped in cross-section and from 20–30 ft wide and 8–12 ft deep. However, the existing width is due mostly to the erosion of the edges. As far as can be ascertained the ditches were originally narrower, probably around twice the depth, or less. Dimensions greater than those just given were by no means uncommon. Probably the largest hillfort ditch was the inner one at Maiden Castle, Dorset, which was 75 ft wide and 27 ft deep at the centre. At both Chalbury (Dorset) and Fridd Faldwyn (Powys) the ditches, dug into sloping ground, were 20 ft deep below their inner edges and,

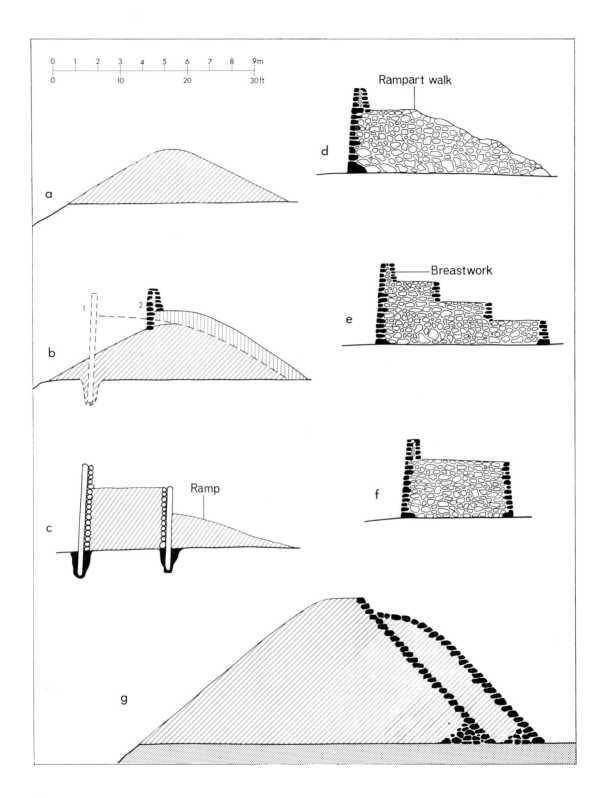

due to erosion, 40–45 ft wide. At Wandlebury (Cambs.), where both original shape and dimensions could be ascertained, the outer ditch was 18 ft wide and 15 ft deep, with very steep sides and a flat bottom 6 ft wide. The ditch at Blewburton (Berks.) is generally similar in profile, but dug into sloping ground, and was, where excavated, 24 ft wide and 17 ft deep with a flat bottom 6–8 ft wide. Because of the difficulties of cutting

through rock, ditches with even wider flat bottoms occur, as at Lyneham (Oxon.) and Okehampton (Devon), where they are 8–10 ft wide in overall widths of 15–20 ft.

Between the ditch and the front of a revetted rampart a space, known as a berm, was normally left, presumably to prevent the undermining of the rampart by erosion of the ditch edge. Berms appear also in other parts of defence systems as will be seen below.

The counterscarp bank is a small bank at the head of the outer slope or scarp (the counterscarp, hence the name) of the ditch. It varies from 10–20 ft wide and

Fig. 3 Hillfort entrances: (a) in a glacis rampart; (b) in a revetted rampart, inturned type.

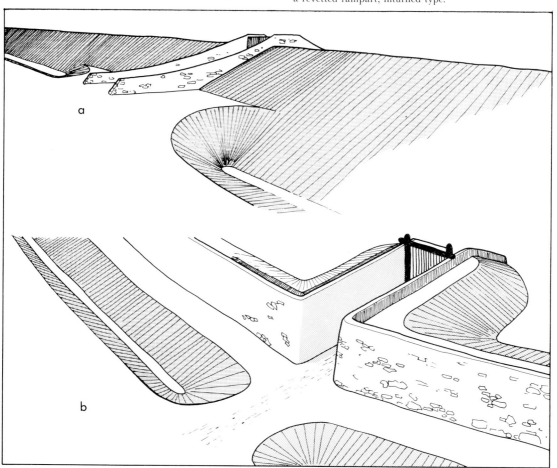

from 2–4 ft high and is a minor obstacle rather than a rampart. It may simply be the result of cleaning out the ditch from time to time. Its general effect is to give added depth to the ditch. In a small number of cases very large counterscarp banks approach rampart dimensions and should probably be classed as such.

Collapse and erosion of ramparts, ditches, berms and counterscarp banks have, over a period of some 2000 years, reduced the original structures to their present-day appearance. As we see them now, the ramparts, whatever their original form, are grass-grown banks of earth or banks of loose stones (depending on the original materials), triangular in cross-section, sloping down to the bottom of the partly filled ditch. Berms have mostly been obscured by the collapse, or eroded, or both, and counterscarp banks were never, in most cases, anything more than small triangular banks anyway. Dimensions vary considerably. At their biggest ramparts can be 20 ft high, even in their collapsed state, with their crests up to 40 ft above the bottom of the partly filled ditch, although the majority of ramparts are less than half this size. In multivallate forts, with two or three closely set ramparts and ditches, the present appearance is that of a series of corrugations running around the slope of the hill.

As in most fortifications entrances often received special attention. These took the form of ramparts arranged in particular ways so as to provide greater protection for the gateways. This being so, entrances can be studied almost as easily from their surface remains as they can be from excavation evidence. In fact, a very large number of hillfort entrances are simply gaps in the rampart, filled originally by a timber gate. One of the commonest ways of elaborating the entrance arrangements was to turn the ramparts on either side of the entrance inwards, parallel to each other, to form a narrow, restricted approach to the actual gateway at the

Fig. 4   Overlapping entrance at Moel y Gaer (Llanbedr), Clwyd.

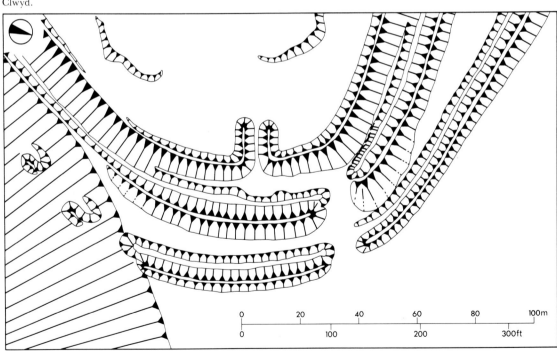

3 Beacon Hill, Hampshire.

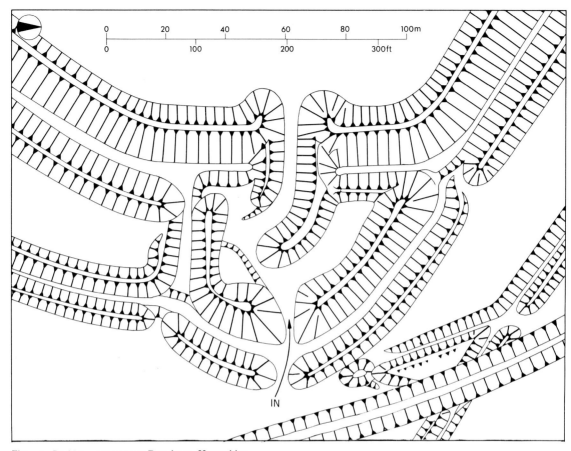

Fig. 5   Barbican entrance at Danebury, Hampshire.

inner end (inturned entrances) (Fig. 3, b).
Less common are out-turned entrances
and inturn/out-turn arrangements.
Sometimes the constricted approach was
achieved by an overlapping arrangement,
the rampart on one side passing in front of
the rampart on the other in the entrance
area (Fig. 4). Protection was sometimes
achieved by single or twin hornworks in
front of the entrance (Pl. 3), and in a
small number of cases there were complete
barbicans or double entrances, an outer
entrance leading into an enclosure which
had to be traversed before the inner
entrance could be reached (Fig. 5).

It is difficult to discuss hillforts any
further in the broad terms used so far
because of the very large numbers

involved, and the variation from
region to region. More particular evidence
is best presented on a geographical basis,
starting with England and Wales, and
making use of the terminology defined
earlier as to situation, defences, layout,
and entrances.

England and Wales The number and broad
distribution of hillforts in England and
Wales have been indicated already.
Within this region there are variations
from area to area in the size, type and
density of sites which will emerge in the
survey to follow. In general terms,
however, it can be stated that the greatest
numbers of the sites are in the western
counties, and reach their peak in Dyfed

and Cornwall. However, this numerical superiority is balanced by the fact that the majority of the sites involved are very small, being mostly only an acre or two in area. Much larger but less numerous hillforts are found in the eastern half of the triangle, that is, southern England, the Cotswolds and the Welsh border country. With this division in size goes also, again in broad terms, a division in types. Most of the larger sites in the eastern zone are of the single-enclosure type, while the smaller, western sites, although still predominantly single-enclosure, include within their area the majority of the multiple-enclosure sites. The hillforts in England and Wales can most conveniently be considered in seven groups: (1) the south-east; (2) Wessex; (3) the Cotswolds; (4) the Welsh Marches;

(5) the Chilterns, midlands and north; (6) the south-west; and (7) south and west Wales.

In south-east England (Surrey, Sussex and Kent) there are some forty hillforts, about half of which are strung out along the South Downs. These are mostly of univallate type and include the Trundle, near Goodwood racecourse, Chanctonbury Ring, the Devil's Dyke, Hollingbury and Cissbury, the latter enclosing some 60 acres and having a very large single rampart and ditch defence. Excavation has shown that the rampart was originally of the revetted type with a timber facing retaining a wedge-shaped mass of earth and chalk behind. The small site of Hollingbury has also been excavated. It too had a revetted rampart, in this case of the box-type, that is, with both front and back timber revetments, and was 7 ft thick, with an additional ramp of earth at the rear. The main exception to the

4   Old Sarum, Wiltshire. In the centre is the great Norman motte, roughly concentric with the Iron Age defences

univallate pattern is Goosehill Camp which is a concentric, multiple-enclosure site which would look much more at home in the south-west than in the south-east. In contrast to the South Downs, the sites in the Weald and North Downs area are mostly multivallate and include two very large sites, Oldbury (Kent) and Dry Hill Camp (Sussex).

The Wessex region (Dorset, Wilts., Hants and Berks.), one of the classic hillfort areas of the British Isles, contains about 150 hillforts, a number of them very large and spectacular, including perhaps the most famous hillfort of all, Maiden Castle (Dorset), extensively excavated in the years before the last war by Sir Mortimer Wheeler. In the area

of Wessex to the east of the River Avon the hillforts are mostly of the univallate type and include such sites as St Catherine's Hill (near Winchester), Beacon Hill (Pl. 3) and Walbury (Hants) and Old Sarum (Pl. 4), Figsbury Rings and Casterley Camp (Wilts.). Excavation has shown that at St Catherine's Hill, Figsbury and Casterley the ramparts were of the sloping-fronted glacis type. At Beacon Hill the main entrance has inturned ramparts and twin curving hornworks on either side. To the west of the Avon there is a high proportion of multivallate sites, including many of what may be termed the Maiden Castle type. These include Eggardon, Hod Hill, Hambledon Hill and Badbury Rings (Dorset), Oldbury (Fig. 6), Bratton Castle,

5   Battlesbury hillfort, Wiltshire.

24

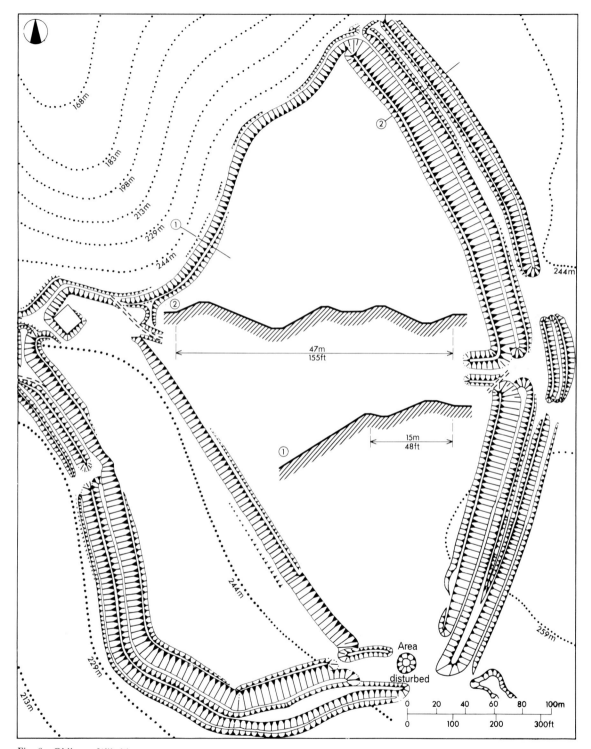

Fig. 6   Oldbury, Wiltshire.

25

Battlesbury (Pl. 5), Yarnbury, Sidbury and Castle Ditches (Wilts.), Castle Ditches and Danebury (Hants) and Cadbury Castle (Somerset). These sites are defended by two, three and four lines of massive ramparts, enclosing areas of from 25–50 acres, and have strongly defended entrances, many of them in the form of outworks forming barbicans or double entrances, as at Badbury Rings or Bratton Castle. In some other sites the overlapping principle has been adopted, as at Hod Hill and Hambledon Hill. At Maiden Castle, the great west entrance is a very complex example of the overlapping principle, while the east entrance is mainly of the barbican type.

The Wessex region also includes a number of multiple-enclosure sites such as Buzbury Rings and Weatherby Castle (Dorset) and White Sheet Castle and Park Hill Camp (Wilts.). Buzbury, Weatherby and Park Hill are of the concentric type (i.e. with one enclosure inside another), but White Sheet Castle is of the annexe type. It stands in a promontory position with three parallel ramparts, about 100 ft apart, cutting off a main and two subsidiary enclosures.

Excavation has produced quite a lot of information about the original structure of the Wessex hillforts. At Bindon on the Dorset coast there was a single rampart, without a ditch, presumably because the fall of the ground made one unnecessary. The rampart had a timber facing, probably originally *c.* 10 ft high, retaining a wedge-shaped mass of earth about 20 ft wide and 6 ft high at the front. Chalbury in the same county had a stone-revetted box-rampart about 20 ft thick with a supporting ramp of earth behind and a deep and wide ditch in front (above). Poundbury, like Bindon, had a wedge-shaped mass of material with a vertical timber front, but on a much larger scale. In front was a berm and a V-shaped ditch. When the rampart collapsed it was rebuilt in hybrid form, a vertical stone revetment standing at the top of the

glacis-like slope formed from the collapsed material. At the same time an outer bank (of simple glacis-type) and a ditch were added, making the site multivallate. At Maiden Castle the first defence was a timber-revetted box-rampart, *c.* 11 ft thick, separated by a berm from a V-shaped ditch. When this collapsed the rampart was rebuilt on glacis lines and the whole site was extended, more than doubling its area. At a later stage again the glacis rampart was greatly increased in size, with stone buttressing at the back, making it over 20 ft high and 50 ft wide with a vertical height of some 60 ft above the bottom of the ditch which was 75 ft wide and 27 ft deep. By this time the site was multivallate, with a massive additional bank, ditch and counterscarp bank on the north side and two additional banks with ditches and a counterscarp bank on the south.

The Cotswold region, centred on Gloucestershire, contains about 100 hillforts, many of them on the steeper, north-western edge of the range, facing the Severn. Few of the multivallate sites are as spectacular as those in Wessex but sites worthy of mention include Kimsbury and Uleybury (Glos.), Worlebury (Avon), and Dolebury (Somerset). Both of the latter were stone-built and much of their visible remains consist of great banks of tumbled stones. Dolebury has a fairly conventional arrangement of two banks and two ditches, but Worlebury, above Weston-super-Mare, in a promontory position, has no less than six banks and ditches forming a band of defences 300 ft deep. Two other lines of bank and ditch cut off two additional enclosures in front of the main defences. Other promontory forts include Crickley Hill, Leckhampton and Haresfield Beacon (all in Glos.). The latter is also a multiple-enclosure site, as is Bredon Hill (Hereford. & Worcs.). Bredon Hill occupies the corner of a high plateau with steep natural slopes on two sides and two widely spaced lines of defences, forming two enclosures, on the two remaining sides. The region includes a number of very large sites: Nottingham Hill (Glos., 130 acres), Bathampton Camp (Avon, 82 acres), and Tedbury Camp (Somerset, 72 acres).

Excavation has yielded some evidence of original structure. At both Chastleton (Oxon.) and Little Solsbury (Somerset) the only structure was a stone-faced box-rampart 20 ft thick, although at the latter site the rampart stood at the head of a steep natural slope. At Bredon Hill (Hereford. & Worcs.) both revetted and glacis ramparts were involved. As first built there was only one rampart, of the glacis type, 45 ft wide and 10 ft high, with a ditch 50 ft wide and 20 ft deep in front. In a second phase an outer bank and ditch were added, 150 ft in front of the first, making it a two-enclosure site. The new rampart had a stone-revetted front retaining a wedge-shaped mass of material 50 ft wide and 10 ft high, separated by a berm from a ditch 35–40 ft wide and 15–16 ft deep.

The Marcher or Welsh border region stretches from the Severn to the North Wales coast (between the Dee and the Conway valleys), and contains some 250 hillforts, a good number of them as large and/or as spectacular as those in Wessex. However, there are also many small sites, found, not surprisingly, on the western side of the region in Wales, where such sites are commonplace. The major group of Marcher hillforts is in southern Shropshire and northern Herefordshire where multivallate forts, many of them with very powerful defences, account for more than half the total number of hillforts. Outstanding among them are Ivington Camp, Wapley Camp and Croft Ambrey (Hereford. & Worcs.), Burfa Camp and Fridd Faldwyn (Powys), and Norton Camp, Bury Ditches (Fig. 7), Caer Caradoc (Clun) (Pl. 6), Caer Caradoc (Church Stretton), Old Oswestry (Pls 2 and 7) and Bury Walls (all in Shropshire). Old Oswestry has no less than seven banks and four or five ditches on its most vulnerable, western side. Special attention was paid to the main entrance, with the

6 Hillfort, Caer Caradoc, Clun, Shropshire.

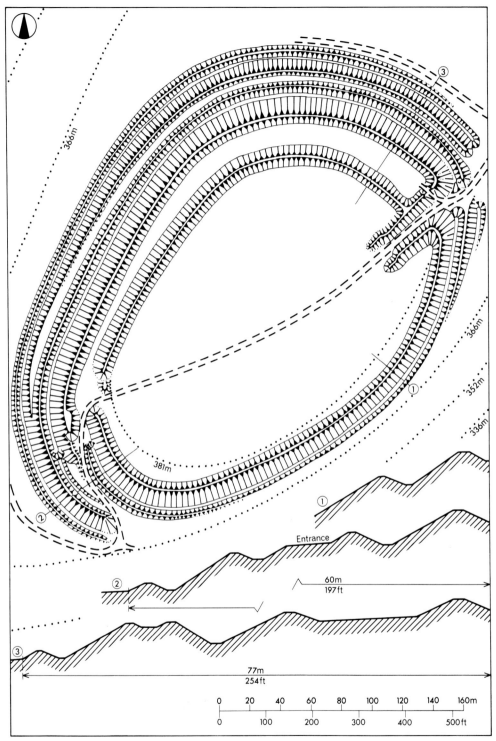

Fig. 7 Bury Ditches, Shropshire.

28

7 Old Oswestry, Shropshire.

entrance passage flanked by ramparts at right angles to the defences. There are complex entrance works also at Wapley Camp, Ivington Camp, Burfa Camp and Caer Caradoc (Clun).

There is another smaller group of multivallate sites in the southern part of the Marcher region, the most notable of which are Llanmelin and Sudbrook Camps (Gwent) and Symond's Yat and Spital Meend (Glos.); the last two are in promontory positions formed by U-shaped bends in the River Wye. There is also a small group at the northern end of the region, sited along the Clwydian range in north-east Wales: Moel Hiraddug; Moel y Gaer (Bodfari); Pen-y-cloddiau; Moel Arthur; Moel y Gaer (Llanbedr); and Foel Fenlli.

The wide range of types in the Marcher

region includes also many multiple-enclosure forts such as the Herefordshire Beacon and the Wrekin (Salop), in both of which there are large annexes to north and south of the main enclosure. The region also includes some very large sites, such as Llanymynech Hill (Powys, 140 acres), Titterstone Clee (Salop, 71 acres), Pen-y-cloddiau (Clwyd, 52 acres) and Credenhill (Hereford. & Worcs., 49 acres).

Excavation in the Marcher hillforts has revealed, among other things, another example of elaborate stone buttressing, similar to Maiden Castle, at the back of the glacis rampart at Sudbrook (Gwent) (Fig. 2, g). It has also uncovered evidence of twin guard chambers in a number of hillfort entrances. These were placed just inside the gates at the inner end of inturned entrances. The guard chambers faced each other across the entrance and were usually c. 15 × 10 ft with one side open to the roadway. Examples are recorded at the Roveries, the Wrekin and Titterstone Clee in Shropshire, and at Pen-y-Corddyn in Clwyd. There is also clear surface evidence of further examples at Pen-y-cloddiau and Moel Arthur in the Clwydian group, at Moel y Gaer (Rhosesmor, Clwyd), and at Caer Caradoc (Clun, Salop). Although they appear occasionally in other regions, most of the examples of guard chambers, known either from excavation or surface observation, come from this region and they appear to be a particular feature of entrances in the northern half of the Welsh Marches.

There is a scatter of sites in the midlands and the north, to the east and north of the regions considered so far. The two main groups are along the north-west edge of the Chilterns and in the southern Pennines. Elsewhere they are widely scattered or non-existent.

In the last two regions to be considered (south and west Wales and south-west England) the overall pattern changes to one of large numbers of very small sites, of coastal promontory forts, and of particular types of multiple-enclosure fort. Of the 300 or so sites in south-west England the most numerous are the small univallate forts, an acre or two in area and often circular in plan, which constitute over one-third of the total. Rather less numerous are multivallate forts of the same size and shape. The most notable example is Chun Castle, a stone-built fort in the Land's End district. For geological reasons coastal promontory forts are fairly common, particularly in Cornwall. Notable examples are Rumps Point and Trevelgue Head (Newquay) (Fig. 8), the latter with no less than seven ramparts, on the north coast, and Dodman Point, Black Head and Rame Head on the south coast.

The most characteristic form of south-western multiple-enclosure site is the concentric fort. At Tregeare Rounds and Killibury (Cornwall) there are near-

circular inner and outer enclosures, c. 300 and 600 ft in diameter respectively. Warbstow Bury (Fig. 1) and Castle-an-Dinas, near St Columb, are on a larger scale but otherwise conform to the concentric plan. In Devon, Clovelly Dykes has no less than six enclosures, the inner two of the concentric type, the outer four in the form of annexes, while at Milber Down there are three concentric enclosures and at least part of a fourth. Many other sites have their additional enclosures in the form of annexes, often covering the entrance like a barbican. In some cases the annexe defences are carried around the defences of the main enclosure, making them multivallate, as at Castle Dore (Cornwall) and Denbury Camp (Devon). In promontory positions two (opposite) sides of any annexe are formed by natural features.

South and west Wales contain about 450 hillforts. The few large sites in the region are mostly in the north and are stone-built, with remains of circular huts. They include Conway Mountain, Tre'r Ceiri, Garn Boduan, Carn Fadrun and Caer y Twr (all in Gwynedd). The main concentration of sites is in the south, in Dyfed and West Glamorgan, where there are large numbers of small, often circular, univallate sites, smaller numbers of corresponding multivallate sites, together with concentric sites, annexe sites and coastal promontory forts, particularly in the south-western extremity. All in all the pattern is very similar to the pattern in south-west England. Some of the outstanding sites of the area are Pen Dinas, near Aberystwyth, Carn Ingli, Foel Trigarn and Gaer Fawr (Dyfed), and the Bulwarks and Summerhouses (South Glam.). There are also good examples of promontory forts at St David's Head and Linney Head (Dyfed) and the Knave near Rhossili (West Glam.).

Hillforts in Scotland There are about 1000 hillforts in Scotland, mostly below the Clyde/Forth line, with particular emphasis

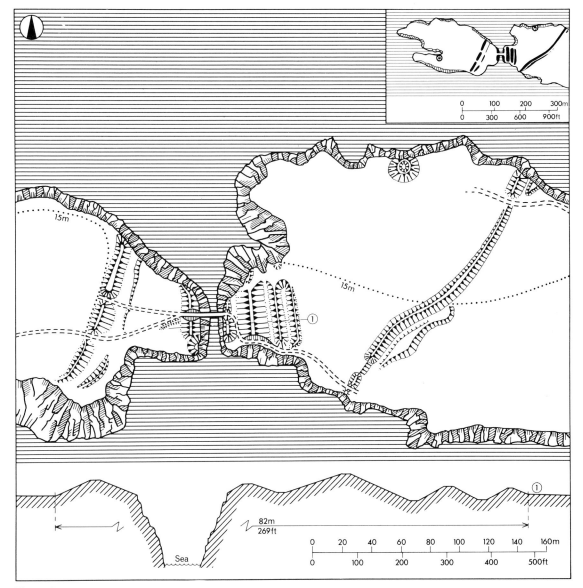

Fig. 8   Trevelgue Head promontory fort, Cornwall.

on the south-east in the counties adjacent to the English border. Included with the Scottish hillforts are those of Northumberland which form part of the same distribution pattern. In their range of sizes and types the Scottish hillforts follow the tradition of south-west England and Wales rather than that of Wessex and the Marches.

In south-eastern Scotland the main areas involved are Dumfries & Galloway, Borders, and east Strathclyde, to which can be added Northumberland. About 500 sites are involved. A high proportion of the sites are small, an acre or two in area, circular or near-circular in plan and with univallate defences, that is, they are very similar to many of the sites in Wales and

8 Dinas Bran, Clwyd. An Iron Age hillfort with a later medieval castle built inside.

south-west England. A much smaller number are of similar size and shape but have multivallate defences, sometimes involving three or four lines of defence, again very much as in the areas just mentioned.

However, not all the sites in south-eastern Scotland are of this type. There are a small number of sites of greater size and complexity. Castle O'er (Dumfries & Galloway) has an inner enclosure c. 500 × 300 ft, a barbican-type entrance and an outer line of defence forming a second enclosure. Birrenswark in the same county is famous for its Roman siege works. The 17-acre hillfort appears to have had two ramparts, now somewhat flattened, and five entrances. The Roman structures consist of two temporary camps immediately below the hill to north and south. Cademuir Hill (Borders) is defended by a stone rampart 10 ft thick

enclosing $5\frac{1}{2}$ acres. Cardrona (also Borders) is one of a number of concentric sites in the county. Two of the larger sites in the county are White Meldon (9 acres, four ramparts), and Whiteside Rig, with a main enclosure 1160 × 330 ft and a smaller, roughly circular one, c. 100 ft in diameter. Torwoodlee hillfort has a later broch (below) just inside its western defences, and Hownam Law (22 acres) and Eildon Hill (39 acres, the largest hillfort in Scotland), both contain large numbers of hut remains, between 150 and 200, and nearly 300 respectively. Woden Law, with four ramparts on the south and east, is notable for its Roman (practice) siege works, consisting of two banks and three ditches, in turn enclosed by more widely spaced works. Other sites include a few of the multiple-enclosure type such as Cockburn Law (two enclosures) and Shannonbank Hill (two concentric enclosures). The oustanding site in

Northumberland is Yevering Bell with a stone rampart enclosing some 13 acres and the remains of 130 huts. Other notable sites in the county include Hambleton Hill, a three-enclosure site, and Harehaugh, with multivallate defences consisting of three banks and two ditches.

In south-west Scotland sites are less numerous than in the south-east and are located for the most part on or near the south-facing coasts of Dumfries & Galloway and the west-facing coast of Strathclyde. The 100 or so sites (both univallate and multivallate) are again mostly small and often circular in plan, except in promontory situations which are fairly common in the region. There are also a few multiple-enclosure sites such as Dungarry and Stroanfreggan.

The remaining Scottish hillforts are scattered up the east coast, from the Forth to John o' Groats. Many of them are of the simple, often circular type encountered already. There are, however, a few more elaborate sites, including the Chesters (Lothian), with complex defences and well-contrived east and west entrances. Traprain Law (32 acres) in the same county has yielded rich finds of metal tools, weapons and ornaments. In Fife, Clatchard Craig (two enclosures) has, at one point, no less than seven banks, while Norman's Law (four enclosures) has stone ramparts 10–16 ft thick. The two outstanding sites in Tayside are the Brown Caterhun (1100 × 1000 ft) and the White Caterhun (1500 × 850 ft), both with complex systems of defences. In Grampian the Barmekin of Echt has two circular inner walls, three earth ramparts and five entrances, only two of which pierce the whole system. Beyond the Moray Firth there is a scatter of sites in Highland county, including Buaile Oscar (900 × 450 ft), defended by a single stone wall.

Hillforts in Ireland There are in Ireland very large numbers of what are generally called 'forts', possibly, according to some accounts, between 30,000 and 40,000, but these include many structures built as late as the Norman Conquest, and in some cases later still. It is, therefore, virtually impossible to isolate the range of prehistoric forts. What can be done is to note the existence of types similar to those encountered already, on the assumption that they are broadly similar in function and date.

There are a few hillforts of the contour or generally similar type, up to 20 acres in area and defended by a single stone rampart or a bank and ditch. These are presumably the Irish equivalent of the larger English univallate forts, and include such sites as Navan, Tara, Dun Ailline and Freestone Hill. At the latter, in Kilkenny, the excavation evidence suggested a date in the fourth century AD, but at Navan, near Armagh, the finds were of the first century AD, that is, broadly in keeping with dates elsewhere in the British Isles.

As in Britain, the existence of coastal promontory forts is dictated by geology, and the majority of those in Ireland are on the south and south-west coasts. About 200 sites are recorded. Their defences consist of one or more ramparts across the neck of the promontory, that is, very much the same pattern as in south-west England and south-west Wales, and it seems feasible to suggest that at least some of the Irish promontory forts were contemporary with those in England and Wales.

Most of the remaining Irish sites come under the heading of ring forts. They include many small circular sites (100–200 ft in diameter) with either simple univallate defences (a bank and ditch or a stone wall), or more complex multivallate defences with two, three and four ramparts. Many of these must be simply Irish versions of the small forts which occur in such large numbers in England, Wales and Scotland.

In view of the very large numbers embraced by the term 'fort' it is difficult to make any unequivocal statement about the Irish position in relation to the rest of the British Isles, but it can at least be seen that, in the larger hillforts, in the coastal promontory forts, in the small circular strongly defended (multivallate) sites, and in the small circular univallate sites, there are clear links with hillforts in other parts of the British Isles, even if the extent of those links cannot as yet be stated in numerical terms.

Function and Date   The last two topics to be considered under the heading of hillforts are function and date. One of the functions traditionally attributed to hillforts is that of a temporary refuge in time of danger, and this is probably true, at least for some hillforts. However, the size, numbers and types involved, the widespread distribution, and the long period during which they were built (seven or eight centuries) make any single function unlikely. It is much more likely that the variations in size, layout and so on reflect, to some degree at least, differences in function. It seems unlikely, for example, that Maiden Castle (Dorset), a huge, complex site, enjoyed the same function as (say) a small, circular, univallate site in Dyfed or that either of them had the same function as a multiple-enclosure site like (say) Clovelly Dykes (Devon). There was probably a whole range of functions which varied from area to area, from period to period and indeed, from type to type.

The existence of a temporary refuge for times of danger implies that the permanent living quarters were somewhere else, presumably in villages below the hillfort, although such settlements have rarely been found. It is quite clear, however, that there are also villages and larger settlements within hillforts as permanent parts of the establishment, and in these must be seen hillforts in the function referred to earlier, that of the town or settlement wall. Whatever they were when first built, sites such as Maiden Castle had, by the end of the Iron Age, just before the Roman Conquest, become substantial urban centres with formidable walls and gates. In economic terms they were probably market towns, and in political terms they were probably provincial capitals. Such sites were never numerous and the type is probably confined to the twenty or so Maiden Castle-type forts in Wessex and a similar number in the remaining regions. There are, however, smaller and simpler sites with fewer (perhaps ten to forty) huts and these must be seen as defended or fortified villages. There is thus a range of permanent settlements which were, as a matter of course, surrounded by defensive walls, and in these must be seen another important function of hillforts.

In northern and western regions, however, many of the forts are much too small to have housed even a village, let alone a town. At most they might have accommodated a hamlet, that is something with, say, three to ten huts and such numbers have been found in them. However, given the buildings required even on a primitive farm, and the fact that the people involved were probably an extended family group (i.e. three generations, grandparents, parents and children), such sites are probably best regarded as fortified farmsteads. They may represent the normal type of Iron Age site in south-west England, south-west Wales, much of Scotland and probably many parts of Ireland, as well, and this may well explain why they are so numerous. Their universal fortification may be a result of the vulnerable western areas in which they were located and the turbulent times in which they were built, or a combination of the two. Whatever the reason, fortified farmsteads would appear to represent another important function of hillforts and one which, in fact, given the very large numbers of small sites mentioned earlier, would account for a considerable proportion of all hillforts.

At least two other types of site call for some comment. The multiple-enclosure sites, particularly the larger ones, must surely be connected in some way with livestock. In a primitive agricultural community much of the tribal wealth must have been bound up in cattle and other stock, and the means to protect that wealth would have been an important factor in the building of the settlement. The separate enclosures of a multiple-enclosure site are surely a means of separating people from animals and various kinds of animals from each other, while at the same time bringing them all within one defensive system. Similarly, the very large sites, 50 acres or more, must surely, in some cases at least, have been large cattle pounds. Many such sites are in upland areas, with one side facing on to a plateau which may have been a summer grazing ground. The hillfort may have been a means of safeguarding the livestock at night, and in times of danger, while at the same time allowing them to continue grazing inside. There is little doubt that cattle raiding took place, and precautions against it are therefore to be expected. Smaller sites may also have been cattle pounds, several of them perhaps being placed around tribal territory so that cattle, wherever they were grazing, would not need to be driven long distances in order to be protected for the night.

One other group, coastal promontory forts, call for some comment in terms of function. Many of them look much too bleak and exposed for permanent settlement, although they could still be temporary refuges in time of danger. However, their location on the coast, directly accessible from a major sea route, makes another function possible, that of trading depots, perhaps used seasonally, when weather conditions suited. They would represent a sort of halfway-house between the population living inland from the coast and the merchants coming by sea from abroad, trading from within a fortified depot which afforded them and their goods some protection from the natives.

Between them the various functions considered above probably cover most of the uses to which hillforts were put. There may well, however, be others which we cannot as yet perceive which will emerge only as a result of future excavation.

The question of dating can be dealt with fairly briefly. The date when hillforts first appeared in the British Isles has been mentioned already, the eighth century BC. Probably at this stage only small numbers were involved. As the numbers grew some of the existing hillforts were strengthened and by about the fifth century BC the addition of outer ramparts transformed some univallate sites into multivallate sites. Probably at the same time or a little later, additional enclosures transformed some sites into multiple-enclosure forts. The further development of some of the multivallate sites (*c.* forty in number) into special multivallate forts of the Maiden Castle type seems to be a matter of the last century or century and a half before the Roman Conquest. This rough timetable applies for the most part to England. Events in western and northern regions and in Ireland were probably delayed by a century or so, possibly more, but until much more evidence is forthcoming, we cannot be certain of the course of events in these areas. What is certain is that ultimately all hillforts in the British Isles will have to be integrated into a single framework of events which makes sense both chronologically and geographically.

Duns

Hillforts of the types described in the last section are rare, although not entirely absent, in northern and western Scotland. Their place is taken, in part, by stone-built fortifications known as *duns*, some 350 of which are scattered down the western side of Scotland, including the Inner and Outer Hebrides. A dun is a small, stone-built, strongly defended fort, often circular or near circular in plan, and up to about 60 ft in internal diameter (Fig. 9). The

Fig. 9 Reconstruction and cross-section of a dun.

rampart is 10–15 ft thick and consists of a solid rubble core and well-built inner and outer faces, often neatly coursed and with a noticeable batter or inward slope. Particular attention was paid to the entrance passage which narrowed in angular fashion to provide door checks for the door which was secured by a bar housed in sockets on either side. Access to the rampart walk was provided by a staircase in the thickness of the wall or by steps projecting from its inner face.

Some or all of the features just described appear in a number of small hillforts and there is, in fact, no hard and fast dividing line between the two. A dun appears to be a specialized form of hillfort, its main distinguishing feature being its small size, usually deemed to be the accommodation for a single family or family group. Those sites intermediate in size (60–120 ft in internal diameter) are either special duns, perhaps for double or special family groups, or simply very small hillforts which have been built on dun principles.

The main concentration of duns is from the northern end of Skye to the southern end of Kintyre. There are about sixty duns in the latter area of which the site near the mouth of Borgadel Water provides an excellent example of the type. It is almost a true circle in plan, with an internal diameter of 42 ft and walls 12 ft thick, preserved up to a height of 6 ft. The outer face of the wall has a pronounced batter. The entrance, on the western side, is 4 ft 3 in. wide internally and 3 ft 6 in. externally, providing two right-angled checks against which the door closed. A large number of duns are similar to this in both size and plan. Any variations are usually the result of particular situations. On promontories, for example, where part of the protection is provided by cliffs, the defences are simply a straight or curving length of rampart facing the landward side, but are exactly the same in structure as in the circular sites.

In addition to promontories, a number of duns are located on *stacks*, column-like masses of rock with flat tops, around the edges of which are the rampart. Dun Fhinn, for example, is near-rectangular in plan (*c.* 45 × 20 ft) with a surrounding wall only 4 ft thick, except near the entrance, where it is 9 ft thick. A number of post-holes about 4 ft out from the inner face are usually interpreted as the remains of lean-to timber buildings and this point will be returned to later.

Dun Kildalloig and Kildonan Bay dun illustrate other features of these structures. Dun Kildalloig conformed to the near-circular plan (internal diameter 45 ft), and had a surrounding rampart 13–16 ft thick. It had, rather unusually, two entrances, one of which (the eastern) had a guard chamber in the thickness of the rampart, opening on to the north side of the entrance passage. There were indications of at least three intra-mural chambers opening on to the central area, one of which was *c.* 11 × 7 ft. Post-holes again suggested that there had been internal timber buildings. At the Kildonan Bay dun an opening just north of the entrance led to twin staircases in the thickness of the rampart which gave access to the rampart walk. South of the entrance there was a narrow passage or gallery running lengthwise along the middle of the wall, dividing it into inner and outer sections.

Galleries of this type, at ground floor level, need not and probably did not imply anything other than an otherwise normal type of dun rampart. There are, however, more elaborate galleries, above ground level, in a number of duns (galleried duns), which appear to be associated with ranges of timber buildings against the inside of the dun wall. Such galleries and associated timber structures present an entirely new picture of duns, a long way removed from the relatively simple circular walled enclosures considered so far, and one which may provide a structural link between duns and the third type of prehistoric fortification to be considered in this chapter, the broch.

Much of the evidence on galleried duns and timber buildings derives from the excavations (1953–7) at the site of Clickhimin in Shetland. There, undefended Bronze Age and Iron Age farmsteads were succeeded by an Iron Age fortification, intermediate in size (138 ft × 125 ft internally) between a dun and a hillfort, with a dun-type rampart 11–12 ft thick. However, the size of the structure is less important in this case than the relationship between the rampart and the domestic structures behind it. The internal structures were built against the inner face of the rampart, with the ceiling of the ground floor rooms level with the rampart walk which was 6–8 ft high (Fig. 10, a). Their front walls, indicated by post-holes and stone pillars, were 17–18 ft in from the rampart, and extended lengthwise for some 85 ft on the north-east side and for about 75 ft on the south-west. For single storey buildings the height of the ordinary dun-rampart was perfectly adequate as a back support. For taller, two storey buildings, however, some addition to the rampart was required to provide a solid surface against which the internal structures could be built. This took the form of a wall (known as a casement wall), built on the inner edge of the rampart walk and extending upwards to a height (7–8 ft) sufficient to provide headroom on the first floor of the building standing against it. Doorways through the casement wall provided access from the upper rooms directly on to the rampart walk. Such upper rooms were probably living quarters, with the lower rooms used for livestock and storage (Fig. 10, b).

One storey and (with the aid of a casement wall) two storey internal accommodation was probably the rule in most duns. However, in a limited number of cases there is evidence of a third storey, built against a correspondingly higher casement wall, with the rampart walk now carried above a gallery (hence galleried duns). This gallery provided communication between the adjacent first floor rooms and, by means of a staircase, between them and the rampart walk above, which was now directly accessible from the second floor rooms (Fig. 10, c). The evidence for this arrangement at Clickhimin is provided not by the main enclosing wall but by a building known as

the blockhouse, just inside the entrance. This is a curving structure about 42 ft long and 14 ft wide, with clear evidence of a covered gallery of the type just described and of internal timber ranges. Other duns, with galleries in the main surrounding walls, are deemed to have had similar associated internal timber structures.

A few other examples of blockhouses are known. There is one of generally similar dimensions on an island in the Loch of Huxter, on Whalsay, and an even larger one (74 ft × 21 ft) near Jarlshof, at the Ness of Burgi (both in Shetland). There is a fourth, smaller possible example on a little island in the Loch of Brindister south of Clickhimin. Two of these blockhouses (Huxter and Ness of Burgi) appear to have had galleries in the same way as Clickhimin and to have been capable, therefore, of supporting three storey timber structures against their inner, casement walls.

Any three storey structure (even if the

Fig. 10 (a-c) The development of the galleried dun; (d) cross-section of a broch tower.

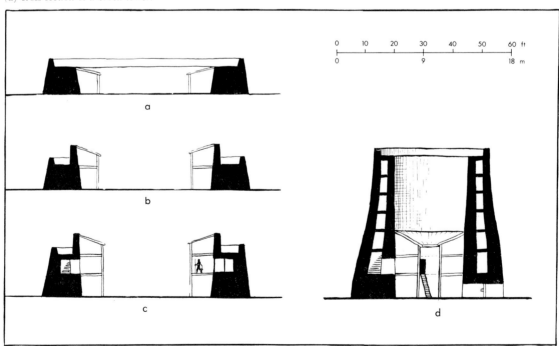

9   Staigue fort, Co. Kerry.

ground floor was used only for livestock) would need to have been in the region of 18–20 ft high and, in fact, casement walls of this height have been recorded in the galleried duns of Dun Ban and Dun Bharabhat in the Hebrides. More specific evidence is recorded at Dun Grugaig in Highland county where the scarcement or ledge which helped to support the second floor was discovered at a point 14 ft high on the casement wall. Allowing a minimum of 6 ft for headroom and 2 ft for the slope of the roof the original height of the casement wall and its associated structures must have been in the region of 22 ft. How numerous such three storey structures were is difficult to say. Drystone buildings are not normally preserved to any great height and in the absence of upper portions it is difficult to make any statement about the height of associated timber buildings. What is clear is that some duns, however few, did develop to (or were built from the start in) the galleried style, supporting three storey internal timber buildings. In summary, the structural range of duns would appear to be as follows: (1) simple duns with no timber structures, perhaps having rooms in the thickness of the rampart; (2) duns with single storey internal structures against the back of the rampart; (3) duns with casement walls with two storey internal timber structures against them; (4) duns with high casement walls, galleries and three storey internal timber structures, the whole being at least 22 ft and probably nearer 25 ft high. The last

10   Grianan of Aileach, Co. Donegal.

group would appear to represent the maximum development of the dun. It has been suggested fairly recently, however, that duns of this type gave rise to the next class of fortification to be considered, brochs. Brochs and duns, and particularly galleried duns, certainly have many features in common, although this does not prove that one was derived from the other. They could well have developed in parallel from some source common to both. Alternatively the comparatively small number of galleried duns could have been an attempt to transform some simple duns into a broch-like structure.

Before dealing with brochs one or two structures in Ireland are worth noting in connection with duns, particularly the larger types such as at Clickhimin. The famous circular stone fort at Staigue in Co. Kerry has a wall 13 ft thick enclosing an area 90 ft in diameter (Pl. 9). There are elaborate stairways up to the top of

the rampart and two chambers in the thickness of the wall. There is a generally similar site at Grianan of Aileach in Co. Donegal, where another 13 ft wall encloses an interior 77 ft in diameter (Pl. 10). The inner enclosure of Dun Oghil in the Aran Islands is of similar character (Pl. 11), as is that of Dun Aengus (also Aran), although the latter is somewhat larger (c. 150 × 130 ft). Quite clearly none of these sites is a dun or a broch. Equally clearly they have enough features in common with them to suggest that they belong to the same general tradition of fortification which, however, found only limited expression in Ireland, and perhaps at a later date.

Brochs

A broch is a circular tower some 40–60 ft in overall diameter, rising to a height of 40–50 ft. The walls are 12–18 ft thick and the interior space 20–30 ft in diameter (Fig. 10, d). In plan this is simply a smaller, more compact version of the dun in which the circular plan has been adopted as standard. The entrances follow the same pattern with door checks and sockets for a door bar. Apart from the generally smaller diameters, it is in the elevation that the main difference between galleried duns and brochs arises. In fact, up to a height of 20–25 ft the two follow very much the same pattern. As in the galleried duns so in the brochs there are scarcements or ledges indicating two floors above ground level, and post-holes in the interiors indicating the front edge of the timber range of buildings. It is above this level that the differences occur. In broch towers the inner casement is carried up for another 20 or 30 ft and is accompanied by an outer casement, forming a double wall with a space between in which there was a staircase which gave access to the top of the tower. Inevitably the uppermost portions have not been preserved and we cannot be certain of the precise arrangements at the top, but presumably the staircase led on to a rampart walk with a breastwork in front, much as in a dun, except for the greater height. In fact, only a few brochs have been preserved to any great height and it is not certain that

11 Dun Oghil, Aran, Co. Galway: ramparts.

12　Broch of Mousa, Shetland.

all of them were of the height suggested earlier (*c.* 50 ft), although a few quite certainly were (Pl. 12). This could be a maximum height in a range varying between perhaps 30 and 50 ft. On the other hand, the uniformity of broch plans may indicate a similar uniformity in height.

About 500 brochs have been recorded, well over half of them in Orkney, Shetland and the northern part of Highland county. The remainder are more widely scattered, mostly in western regions, but with some in the south, in the Lowland zone, as well.

Among the features which appear in brochs are guard chambers, basal galleries and mural chambers, all of which are contrived in the thickness of the walls. Guard chambers (round, oval, sub-rectangular or rectangular), either singly or in pairs, are often placed so that their doorways open on to the entrance passage just behind the doorchecks. Basal galleries, that is, galleries at ground floor level, are not common in brochs and where they were built appear to have proved a weakness, for there is evidence of the early collapse of some of them. Mural chambers (rooms in the thickness of the wall), however, are fairly common. They vary in shape in much the same way as guard chambers. The majority of brochs have only one or two such chambers; the remainder have three, four and (in one case only), five mural chambers. From one of the mural chambers, usually to the left of the entrance, rose the staircase, between the walls, rising to the top of the tower. Occasionally there were two staircases, and occasionally also the staircase started at first floor level, with a ladder against the timber range providing access from ground level. The inner and outer walls of the tower were linked by horizontal bonding slabs which formed the floor of a series of superimposed galleries.

At Clickhimin the dun-style fortification was succeeded by a broch tower, some 65 ft in overall diameter, with walls $17\frac{1}{2}$ ft thick (at the base) and a central space 30 ft in diameter. There were two oval mural chambers, one 13 ft × 5 ft and one 12 ft 9 in × 5 ft 6 in. Access to the staircase was at first floor level, which was 6 ft high, the height of the scarcement or ledge on the inner wall.

Only half of the broch at Jarlshof in Shetland is preserved but what remains indicates that it was slightly smaller than Clickhimin (diameter, 60 ft, walls, 17 ft thick, interior, 25 ft in diameter). It had an attached, roughly D-shaped walled courtyard on its west side, c. 130 ft long and 75 ft wide. There were circular guard chambers at the entrance and an oval mural chamber, 15 ft × 5 ft. Again the mural staircase began at first floor level.

The brochs at Gurness and Midhowe in Orkney, of similar dimensions to Jarlshof, both have basal galleries of the type mentioned earlier. These are linked with one or both of the twin guard chambers which each site has on either side of the entrance. As pointed out earlier, such galleries appear to have weakened the broch structure and there is evidence that Gurness collapsed fairly soon after it was built.

Nothing has been said so far about the circumstances in which both duns and brochs came to be built. They belong to the Iron Age period which began in the British Isles c. 500 BC. However, at least in the north and west (the dun and broch areas) the earliest part of the period seems to have been peaceful, judging by a number of open, undefended settlements. By c. 300–200 BC, however, hillforts were probably already in existence in the Lowland zone, built by the Caledonii who, as will be seen below, later turned

their aggressive energies against the Romans. It was possibly in response to the threat of the expanding Caledonii that duns and brochs were built in the formerly peaceful regions of the north and west. If this is so then the beginnings of dun and broch architecture can be placed somewhere between 200 and 100 BC.

In spite of their elaborate structure broch towers appear to have had a relatively short history. By c. AD 80–100 many of them appear to have gone out of use. This is the date of the Roman penetration of Scotland which resulted eventually in the Hadrianic and Antonine frontiers, further to the south. The Caledonii appear then to have turned their attentions to the richer Roman preserves, leaving the north and west again to their own devices. The brochs fell into disuse and open settlements developed around their remains. The less elaborate duns may have persisted somewhat longer. They were less specialized than the brochs and more easily adaptable to peaceful existence. They were, in any case, geographically closer to the Caledonii who could probably still provide occasional trouble so that wholesale abandonment was unlikely, at least in the short term.

2 Fortification in Roman and Dark Age Britain

The Roman Conquest of AD 43 marked the introduction to Britain of a whole new range of fortifications, quite different from the hillforts, duns and brochs of the last chapter. As the conquest progressed hillforts, which probably formed the last points of resistance, were gradually reduced and rendered ineffective as defences, except apparently in north-west Wales where some were allowed to remain for reasons of local defence. Outside the area of the conquest, in northern and western Scotland, prehistoric fortifications survived, although as pointed out earlier, the brochs seemed to have come to an end fairly quickly for reasons connected with, although not directly a result of, the Roman presence. The new fortifications were the work of an efficient, highly organized, professional army which built defence works to a standard pattern, wherever they were in the Roman Empire—Syria, North Africa, Germany or Britain. This standard, developed over a long period, was firmly established by the time the Romans invaded Britain in AD 43, and the uniformity of plan will be clearly evident as the various types of establishment are described.

The standard shape of a Roman military enclosure is that of a rectangle with rounded corners, often described as a playing-card shape (Fig. 11, a–c).

Sometimes the card is rather long and narrow, at others almost square. The main entrance (the *porta praetoria*) is at the middle of one of the shorter sides and leads into a T-shaped arrangement of internal roads which is the key to the whole plan. At the head of the T is the headquarters area, with two further gates to left and right in the two long sides. Parallel to the head of the T (the *via principalis*), and behind the headquarters area, was another road running across the camp (the *via quintana*); in some cases there were gates at the ends of this road also, but this was by no means universal. At right angles to this road was the last major road of the arrangement, the *via decumana*, leading to the *porta decumana*, at the opposite end of the site to the main entrance. There are thus either four or six entrances, and this is not merely a matter of size. As will be seen later, some of the larger sites have only four entrances, while some of the smaller have six. Much of the interior space was occupied by the living quarters of the troops, but the central area, between the *via principalis* and the *via quintana*, was normally given over to the commandant's and other officers' houses, and to such things as granaries, workshops, baths. There were, indeed, variations from site to site, but these were far outweighed by the regular features which were repeated time after time in thousands of Roman military establishments throughout the Empire.

The playing-card plan and the internal layout were developed during the period of the Roman Republic—in broad terms, the centuries BC—when tented camps were the rule for both temporary and permanent purposes. Gradually, however, as the conquered territories grew and military responsibilities became more complex, tented camps, although retained for marching and campaign purposes, were replaced, for garrison duties, by fortresses and forts (the word camp is no longer appropriate), built at first of earth and timber and later—in broad terms from c. AD 100 on—of stone. There are thus three types, all of which are well represented in Britain: the temporary or semi-permanent (tented) camp, used when marching and on campaigns; the fortress; and the fort. The two latter types, and the distinction between them, call for some further comment.

The term fortress is usually reserved for *legionary* establishments (Fig. 11, a), the term fort for those staffed by *auxiliary* troops (Fig. 11, b), and these two terms indicate the two major sections of the Roman army. One section, the legions, was composed of highly trained professional troops, mostly heavy infantry but with a small contingent of cavalry, all of them Roman citizens. These were the crack troops of the army. The other section, the auxiliaries, were native troops raised locally in the various frontier provinces (Spain, North Africa, Syria, etc.), with Roman officers but usually retaining their own native weapons and equipment. The auxiliary units included both infantry and cavalry formations, together with a number in which infantry and cavalry were combined.

As their name indicates, the legionary troops were organized in legions, between 5000 and 6000 strong (a division in modern military terms), and were housed as a single group in a legionary fortress or barracks. At any one time there were about thirty legions in the Roman army, providing a combined force of between 150,000 and 180,000 high grade troops. The auxiliary troops were organized in smaller groups which varied somewhat in size (below), but were rarely more than a thousand strong. They were housed in auxiliary forts which, although much smaller than the legionary fortresses, were nevertheless laid out on the same lines. Legionary fortresses and auxiliary forts, together with a number of smaller establishments, represent the permanent quarters of the Roman army. When on the march or on campaign both legionaries and auxiliaries made use of temporary or semi-permanent tented camps, varying in size according to need.

Apart from the structures just mentioned Roman fortifications in Britain also included frontier works, town defences and a group of late forts, known as the forts of the Saxon Shore. The whole group will be considered under the following headings: (1) temporary camps; (2) legionary fortresses; (3) auxiliary forts, fortlets and towers; (4) frontier works (Hadrian's Wall, the Antonine Wall); (5) forts of the Saxon Shore; (6) town defences.

Temporary Camps

It was standard Roman military practice to build a perimeter earthwork around every camp, even for a single night's halt. The earthwork was, in most cases, of no great size and consisted of a ditch on average 6 ft wide and 3 ft deep with the earth thrown inwards to form a bank of similar dimensions. Wooden stakes, of which two or three were carried by each soldier for this purpose, were driven into the top of the bank to form a palisade. Special attention was paid to the entrances. A common feature was the *tutulus*, a free-standing length of bank and ditch placed directly in front of the entrance to prevent a direct approach

(Fig. 11, d). An alternative arrangement was the *clavicula*, a curving extension of the rampart projecting inwards or outwards which again acted as a check on direct access. The presence of these features is usually a clear indication that an earthwork is Roman and, further, that it is of the temporary, marching camp type, since *tutuli* and *claviculae* are rarely found in permanent fortresses and forts.

Although the ideal of the playing-card shape was always the aim, temporary camps show greater variation from the standard than do the permanent establishments. This was clearly a time factor. At the end of a day's march there was not much time to search for the perfect site. The surveyors, whose job it was to mark out the camp in advance of

the main body of troops, would have to make do with what was available, and this often meant that the shape and internal layout had to be adjusted to conform to the local terrain. Nevertheless, the desired shape and layout were always kept in mind and a Roman marching camp was never an untidy, irregular shape. The rounded corners and the straight sides were always retained, even if the opposite sides were not always parallel and even if, occasionally, there were more than four sides to the layout. The position of gates indicates that in most cases the T-shaped arrangement of roads was adhered to. All in all, in spite of the fact that it was a temporary structure, the Roman marching camp still conveys the impression of order, tidiness and discipline which were such an essential part of Roman military thinking.

As indicated earlier, temporary camps varied, and had to vary, in size according to the military unit involved, an auxiliary

Fig. 11   Outline plan of Roman fortifications: (a) a legionary fortress, based on Chester; (b) an auxiliary fort, based on Fendoch, Tayside; (c) a fortlet; (d) a large marching camp (Featherwood West, Northumberland), with suggested layout of internal roads.

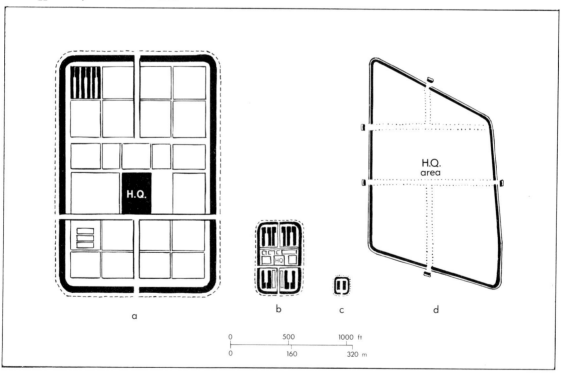

H.Q.

H.Q.
area

a

b

c

d

0   500   1000 ft

0   160   320 m

46

cohort (480 men), a legion (5–6000 men), or even several legions when a large scale operation was being carried out. It has been calculated that a camp about 900 ft square would be required to house a legion on the march, and camps of this size are more common than permanent legionary establishments which were comparatively few. But where large scale operations were involved (e.g. Agricola's invasion of Scotland, or the punitive campaigns by Septimius Severus, again in Scotland, in AD 208–10), several legions might be employed, together with auxiliary units, and the requisite marching camps would need to be even larger than the 900 ft square mentioned above. A camp at Featherwood West (Northumb.) (Fig. 11, d) was c. 1600 × 1100 ft and could have comfortably accommodated two legions (or an equivalent number of auxiliary troops); another at Raedykes (Grampian) was 2300 × 1800 ft measured along the axial roadways and could, on the same basis, have contained five legions, if indeed five legions were ever available in Britain. Even for the initial conquest only four legions were used, so that presumably the army housed in Raedykes consisted at most of two legions supported by auxiliary troops, both infantry and cavalry, for which latter more than the usual space would have been required. In addition, such a large camp may have acted as a supply base for a campaign so that not all of the space would have been devoted to troop accommodation. Only very large marching camps have been mentioned so far. There were, of course, many sites smaller than the 900 ft square type mentioned earlier, reflecting the movement of units other than a legion, perhaps an auxiliary cohort (480 or 800 men), or several such together.

The bulk of Roman temporary camps are of the type just described, camps built for immediate use while on the march or on campaign, although in the latter case occupation might stretch over a matter of days or even weeks in one place. There are, however, one or two other types which come into the temporary category. There are, in the first place, practice camps, marching camps built by troops as part of their training so that on active service they could construct an overnight camp as a matter of routine, with some experience behind them. Such practice camps have been identified in the neighbourhood of Haltwhisle Burn (on the Stanegate, south of Hadrian's Wall), and at Castell Collen (Powys) and Tomen-y-mur (Gwynedd) in Wales.

Another group of temporary works were for longer use than the few weeks mentioned above. A particular duty might call for a unit to be in one camp for a matter of months or even a year, so that while a permanent fort was still not called for, something more than a marching camp was desirable, and such works are normally designated semi-permanent. Their chief characteristic was that their surrounding earthworks were on a larger scale than the normal marching camp and approached the size of the ramparts of permanent forts. However, they lacked the internal buildings of a fort (although this cannot be seen from surface examination alone), and their entrances nearly always had *tutuli* or *claviculae* characteristic of a temporary (even if rather long-term) structure. The rampart of such a fort could be up to 20 ft wide and perhaps originally 8 ft high, with a timber palisade and rampart walk at the top, or even have a complete timber revetment or facing giving it a vertical front. In some cases the ramparts of such camps were turf built, like those of many permanent forts in the first century AD. Good examples of semi-permanent camps are known at Chew Green (Northumb.) and Cawthorn (Yorks.). Roman siege works were also of the semi-permanent type, the most famous examples being the two camps below the native hillfort of Birrenswark (Dumfries & Galloway). There are also practice siege works at Woden Law hillfort in Borders county, illustrating again the thoroughness of Roman training.

Legionary Fortresses

Once the initial conquest was over the legionary complement of the British garrison settled down at three legions, with permanent bases at York, Chester and Caerleon (Gwent) (Fig. 11, a). In the early years of the occupation there had been fortresses at Lincoln and Gloucester. There is, in addition, one legionary fortress at Inchtuthil in Tayside, Scotland, which was built and very quickly abandoned in the years AD 83–7. There are thus remains of only six legionary fortresses in Britain, only three of which were occupied over a long period. In view of the long occupation, in broad terms some three centuries, it is appropriate to say something about the nature and function of these large military bases, and particularly about the implications of the word fortress. This suggests something very strong, with a defensive aspect, rather like a medieval castle which was built, on the whole, with the idea of keeping people out. But for the size of legionary bases (c. 50 acres), their defences are not particularly impressive, mainly because they were not conceived in defensive terms. The Roman legions would never wait within a fortification to be attacked. They were at their most formidable fighting as a highly mobile, disciplined force in the open. The base they issued from was, in fact, more in the nature of a barracks than a fortress. Obviously defences were required but they were not the over-riding consideration. The size of the legion, up to 6000 men, was much greater than would be required for a purely defensive role; the 6000 or so feet of rampart in a legionary fortress would allow only 1 ft of rampart space per man, which is gross overmanning. Probably a third or even a quarter of that number would be adequate for purely defensive purposes but, as already indicated, defence

was not the primary function. The term fortress is probably now too well established to be changed, but the function of these legionary bases as barracks should always be kept in mind.

Although it was occupied only briefly, Inchtuthil in Scotland is the most informative of legionary fortresses in Britain because, unlike all the others, it was never subsequently built over. It was extensively excavated by the late Professor (Sir) Ian Richmond in 1952, and displays the layout characteristic of all Roman legionary fortresses wherever they occur in the Empire from Syria to Scotland and from North Africa to the Danube. The defences consisted of a 5 ft thick stone wall, backed up by a turf rampart, 13 ft thick, with a ditch 20 ft wide and 6½ ft deep in front. The double gateways with twin flanking towers were timber-built. These defences enclosed an area of 53 acres, very nearly square in plan (1565 × 1520 ft). From the main entrance (*porta praetoria*) on the south side a roadway ran in towards the centre of the fortress for 600 ft, where it formed a T-junction with the roadway linking the eastern and western entrances, the *via principalis*, some 1500 ft long. Beyond the *via principalis*, virtually at the centre of the fortress, was the headquarters building, some 150 ft square in its classic position according to standard Roman military practice.

Much of the remaining space within the fortress was occupied by barrack blocks, the arrangement of which reflects the organization of the legion. Each legion was divided into ten cohorts and there are ten groups of barrack blocks, one group for each cohort. Each cohort, except the first cohort, the senior cohort of the legion, was made up of six centuries, each composed of 80 men, under the command of a centurion. Although the term century means literally a hundred, and presumably the unit originally contained a hundred men, by the time of the invasion of Britain the complement had been reduced to 80, although the long-established term century was retained. The 480 men of each cohort were housed in the six barrack blocks which each group contained, one century per block. The men were housed in groups of eight each in a pair of rooms with the more elaborate centurion's quarters at one end. Each barrack block was some 280 ft long and 40 ft wide.

This arrangement accounts for nine of the ten cohorts and fifty-four of the sixty-four barrack blocks. The first cohort, however, consisted of double centuries (i.e. 160 men instead of 80), but had only five of them instead of the usual six (i.e. 160 × 5 = 800, instead of 480). Its ten barrack blocks occupy a special position just behind the *via principalis* and to the west of the headquarters building. Because its five centurions were the most senior of the legion they had more lavish quarters than the other centurions and their five houses can be seen between the barrack blocks and the *via principalis*. The one nearest the headquarters is larger again and presumably housed the most senior centurion in the legion (the *primus pilus*). There are thus sixty-four barrack blocks at Inchtuthil and all of them can be clearly seen on the plan.

A legion, however, needed many other buildings besides barrack blocks and a headquarters to enable it to function properly. The largest building (in area) at Inchtuthil was the legionary hospital, *c.* 300 × 200 ft, with wards on either side of a central corridor and an open central courtyard. The workshop was also arranged around a central courtyard and was *c.* 200 ft square. There were also a drill hall, six granaries, four officer's houses, and a number of considerable open spaces, presumably intended for buildings which had not been begun when the site was abandoned. One of these, in the open space to the east of the headquarters building, was the commandant's house, always adjacent to the headquarters. Immediately to the south of the *via principalis* are four officer's houses,

presumably for four of the normal six military tribunes in a legion, and there is space for at least two more, apparently never started. The legion also contained a small cavalry unit, the barracks and stables for which were just to the west of the headquarters building, between it and the quarters of the first cohort. There were, in addition to all of these, many smaller buildings fulfilling the many different functions required by a military community of nearly 6000 men.

Inchtuthil is invaluable not only because it was possible to uncover the complete plan but also because it was all of a piece, of one period, with nothing in the way of additions. The picture of the other legionary fortresses in Britain is much less satisfactory. Lincoln and Gloucester were occupied for relatively short periods (20–30 years) in the early days of the conquest. At Lincoln it is known that the defences were of earth revetted with timber enclosing an area of $41\frac{1}{2}$ acres, somewhat small by legionary standards. After it was abandoned as a legionary fortress (in favour of York) Lincoln became a *colonia*, a settlement for retired legionaries, and the remains of the legionary establishment lie buried beneath the remains of the settlement, the defensive walls of which exactly follow the lines of the fortress walls.

In AD 71, as part of the campaign to subdue the Brigantes of northern England, the Ninth Legion was moved from its existing base at Lincoln to a new base at York (Eburacum), where the legionary fortress built to house it became one of the three permanent legionary bases during the remaining centuries of the Roman occupation. Although the line of the defences and of the principal roads have been established, not much is known of the internal buildings. The fortress measured 1590 × 1370 ft and, like all the early fortifications in Britain, was originally defended by an earth and timber rampart. This was, however, replaced by a stone wall inserted in front of the earth bank in the years AD 107–8, in

13 Remains of the north wall (lower courses) of the legionary fortress at Chester (Deva).

a period when many other originally timber-built defences were being replaced in stone. The stone wall was itself rebuilt *c.* AD 200, possibly as a result of destruction during the attempt of Clodius Albinus to become Emperor. In a later period, *c.* AD 300, a series of eight large projecting towers was added to the south-west side of the fortress, facing the River Ouse; the remains of one of these, the Multangular Tower at the west corner of the fortress, is still a prominent visible feature in a park adjacent to the river, and the existence of a similar corner bastion has been established at the south angle of the fortress. The headquarters building at the centre of the fortress lies beneath York Minster. Recent work on the foundations of the cathedral, however, has provided some details of the Roman headquarters which was stone-built and

appears to have been *c.* 325 ft long and 290 ft wide, considerably larger than the one described earlier at Inchtuthil. It was burnt down and restored three times in its history, the first two occasions possibly being the result of events in AD 197 (above), and 296, when another attempt was made to usurp Imperial power. Remains of four barrack blocks, each *c.* 200 ft long, have been discovered along the south-west side of the fortress.

An early fortification at Wroxeter (Salop) was succeeded by one at Chester (Deva), *c.* AD 78; the site at Chester may already have been occupied by an auxiliary fort. The legionary fortress covered some 56 acres (1950 × 1360 ft), somewhat larger than the usual 50 acres, and the extra space may have been required for naval personnel, who could well have been based on the River Dee (Fig. 11, a). There is rather more detail of the internal buildings than at York, although the picture is still far from complete. The plans of five complete groups of barrack blocks for five of the ten cohorts have been established at the back of the fortress, and there are other isolated barrack blocks east and west of the headquarters buildings. The two to the west are presumably part of the ten needed for the first (double) cohort. The headquarters building was of similar size to the one at York (310 × 250 ft), the most prominent feature of which was a colonnaded cross-hall, the bases for the columns of which have been recovered. In other parts of the fortress were the remains of the legionary bath-house and of three granaries, side by side, each *c.* 160 × 50 ft. Chester seems to have escaped the destruction which took place in York in AD 197, but not the one a century later in AD 296. There is clear evidence of rebuilding late in the third century when

a large number of inscribed and sculptured stones were found in the structure of the wall, an indication of the urgency with which the reconstruction was carried through (Pls 13 and 14).

Like Lincoln, Gloucester became a *colonia* when the legion there was moved to a new base at Caerleon (*Isca*), *c.* AD 64–5. Caerleon is just over 50 acres in area (1620 × 1350 ft). The original defences were a clay bank revetted front and back with timber, but later a 5 ft thick stone wall was inserted into the bank, as at other sites early in the second century. There was a single ditch in front. Inside more than half the barrack blocks have been uncovered, either in whole or in part, and show that Caerleon conformed to the standard plan. In particular, the ten barrack blocks of the first (double) cohort have been located in the usual position, immediately adjacent to the headquarters. In front of them were three

14   Chester: Roman turret at the south-east angle of the legionary fortress.

of the five houses of the senior centurions. Other internal buildings located included a drill hall, the legionary hospital and a bath-house. The dimensions and layout of the headquarters building have not been established.

The four major legionary establishments in Britain (Inchtuthil, York, Chester and Caerleon) were all begun within a period of twelve years (AD 71–83), and this is quite evident in their plans. Although there are inevitably variations from site to site, it is quite clear that each one was planned with the same broad considerations in mind.

Auxiliary Forts

The forts which housed the auxiliary (i.e. non-legionary) troops were much smaller than the legionary fortresses, being on average only about one-tenth of their size, *c.* 5 acres as opposed to 50 acres (Fig. 11, b). On the other hand, they were very much more numerous, over 200 being recorded in Britain, although not all of these would have been in use at the same time. The auxiliary forces included both infantry and cavalry, each of which was organized into units of different sizes, and the size and layout of auxiliary forts reflect these differences. The infantry were organized into cohorts consisting of either six or ten centuries, i.e. either 480 or 800 men. The cavalry were organized into *alae* (wings, singular *ala*), each containing 16 or 24 *turmae* of 30 men each (either 480 or 720 men in all), although the latter size of formation was rather rare. Although the numbers are very similar to those of infantry units, a cavalry fort had also to provide accommodation for the horses so that space had to be allowed for stables. In broad terms a fort 400 × 400 ft will accommodate an ordinary infantry cohort (480 men), one 600 × 400 ft will accommodate a double infantry cohort (800 men) or an ordinary unit of cavalry (480 men and their horses), while a fort around 700 × 600 ft would be required for the larger cavalry unit (720 men and horses).

In plan and layout auxiliary forts are a scaled down version of legionary fortresses. They have the same playing-card shape, the same disposition of gates and internal roadways, and the same location for the headquarters building and the commandant's house. The reduced space and the smaller garrison called for far fewer buildings, and in most cases the internal structures consisted of barrack blocks, stables, workshops, granaries, a hospital, a headquarters building and a commandant's house, and not much else. The variations on the basic theme of auxiliary forts will emerge in the examples to be considered below.

The auxiliary forts at Gelligaer (Mid Glam.) and Balmuidy (Strathclyde), the latter forming part of the Antonine Wall, both accommodated standard infantry cohorts of 480 men. Gelligaer (built in AD 103–12) conforms closely to the standard given earlier (400 × 400 ft for 480 men), being 404 × 385 ft to the outside of the rampart. This consisted of a mass of clay retained between an outer stone wall, 4 ft thick, and an inner wall, 3 ft thick, with an overall thickness of 20 ft, and a frontal ditch 20 ft wide and 7 ft deep. There were four double gateways set between twin towers, and twelve single towers, 20 ft square, at the corners, and midway between each corner and each gateway. The main entrance was on the north-east and on each side of the entrance roadway was a pair of barrack blocks, 145 ft long and 35 ft wide. There were two other similar barrack blocks at the back of the fort, making six in all, the accommodation for six centuries of 80 men each, 480 men in all. The remaining buildings were the headquarters and the commandant's house, in their standard positions, two granaries and six other buildings not certainly identified. Some at least of these were probably for storage, but one of them, alongside the headquarters, presumably had some more important function, although it did include the camp latrine. Attached to the fort on the south-east side was an annexe (*c.* 360 × 225 ft) containing, among other things, a large bath-house and surrounded on three sides by a simple wall and ditch.

Balmuidy, one of only two stone-built forts on the Antonine Wall, is somewhat larger than Gelligaer (460 × 413 ft). Its defences consisted of a stone wall 7 ft thick at the base, backed by an earth rampart 20 ft wide, with an arrangement of three ditches in front on the south and west sides and two on the east side. The north side forms part of the Antonine Wall, where the main entrance is located. Again there are remains of four barrack blocks in the forward part of the fort and two in the rear, providing the accommodation for the 480-man cohort. However, as the dimensions indicate, the space was fairly generous for a 480-man cohort and it may

be that in an earlier phase there were additional barrack blocks to enable the fort to house an 800-man cohort.

Housesteads, one of the best known and most accessible forts on Hadrian's Wall, with its foundations preserved and visible, is a good example of a fort designed for an 800-man infantry cohort (built *c.* AD 125). Unlike Gelligaer and Balmuidy which are square or nearly square in plan, Housesteads is long and narrow (610 × 367 ft), with one of its long sides forming part of Hadrian's Wall. There is no ditch on this side since the fort and the Wall stand above a steep natural slope. Its main defence was a stone wall, 5 ft thick, backed by a clay rampart 15 ft wide, with only two short lengths of ditch, no longer visible, at the eastern and western ends. The front and rear of the fort contained between them twelve long buildings, ten of which were barrack blocks for the garrison

15 Replica of a section of Hadrian's Wall, Vindolanda.

($10 \times 80 = 800$ men), the other two being a mess hall and a workshop. The central section of the fort contained the headquarters, the commandant's house, the hospital, two granaries, and one or two other buildings, the use of which is uncertain.

Fendoch (Tayside, built by the governor Agricola in AD 78–84) is an earlier example of an 800-man cohort fort which is invaluable in that it was never subsequently rebuilt. It is similar to Housesteads in size and plan (598×330 ft), although as in all forts of this early period timber rather than stone was the main raw material. The rampart, *c.* 17 ft thick, was built of turf, surmounted by a rampart walk and a frontal palisade of timber, with an overall height of probably *c.* 18 ft. In front was a ditch 13 ft wide and 6 ft deep, with a second smaller ditch in front on the north-eastern side. The

internal buildings were timber-framed with the panels filled with wattle and daub. There were four 80-man barrack blocks in the front part of the fort and six in the rear ($10 \times 80 = 800$ men). In the central sector were the headquarters, the commandant's house, the hospital, two granaries, and one or two miscellaneous buildings, possibly storerooms or workshops.

Chesters, like Housesteads, forms part of Hadrian's Wall and, with much of its structure still visible as foundations or low walls, is an example of a cavalry fort corresponding to the single cohort infantry forts (Fig. 12, a). It measures 582×434 ft and was defended by a 5 ft thick stone wall backed by an earth rampart, with double ditches all around, and six entrances. Internally it had eight barrack blocks, each housing two *turmae* (30×2), making a total of 480 men ($30 \times 2 \times 8$). Matching the eight barracks were eight

Fig. 12 Hadrian's Wall: (a) a cavalry fort, based on Chesters; (b) an infantry fort, based on Carrawbrough.

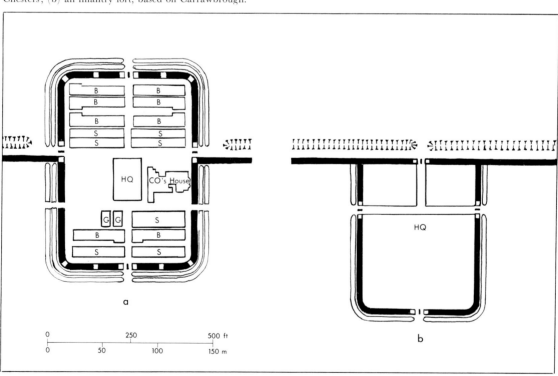

16 Hardknott Roman fort, Cumbria.

stable blocks, arranged either singly or as double blocks. The remaining space was occupied by the headquarters, the commandant's house and private bath-house, and granaries, although the use of part of the central area, to the west of the headquarters, is uncertain.

Other auxiliary forts which can be mentioned here include three in Gwynedd, Caerhun, Caernarvon and Pen Llystyn. Caerhun was similar in plan and layout to Gelligaer but somewhat larger, in order to accommodate a mixed unit, an auxiliary cohort which was part mounted. Caernarvon, of which much is still visible,

was larger again (550 × 450 ft), and probably housed a double cohort of 800 men. Pen Llystyn contained six barrack blocks in the main part of the site (6 × 80 = 480 men), but the back of the fort, separated from the rest by a gateway, contained five more barrack blocks and a building of unknown use, perhaps the accommodation for a separate or special unit of some sort.

Not all auxiliary forts were of the dimensions just quoted. On average the auxiliary forts on the Antonine Wall were smaller than those on Hadrian's Wall which conformed to standard unit sizes.

Many of the Antonine Wall forts were *c.* 3 acres in area and the smallest, Rough Castle, only 1 acre (*c.* 260 ft square), having apparently space for only four barrack blocks, and those smaller than usual. Although the garrison was nominally an infantry cohort of 480 men, not all of them could have been housed in the fort. There must have been detachments elsewhere, with Rough Castle serving as the base depot. There was a fort of generally similar size at Brough in Derbyshire (350 × 290 ft). Again the barrack blocks were fewer and smaller than usual and the fort could not have accommodated the whole of the garrison, the first cohort of Aquitanians, some of whom must have been accommodated separately. Brough was defended by the usual stone wall (5 ft thick), backed by a 15 ft clay bank.

The outer defences at Brough consisted of three ditches with an overall width of about 80 ft, and double and treble ditches have been noted already at some of the sites discussed above. There are, however, a number of sites with even more elaborate ditch systems. Birrens in Dumfries & Galloway had no less than five closely spaced ditches, with an overall width of 125 ft, and there was a similar number at Ardoch in Tayside. At Whitley Castle, Northumberland, there were three or four ditches for most of the circuit and no less than seven on the south-west side, with a depth (front to back) of around 160 ft. Such elaborate ditch systems were presumably a reflection of the turbulent times in which the fort involved was built, or were meant to compensate for some vulnerable or blind spot in the defences.

Even the smallest fort mentioned above, Rough Castle (1 acre) was still noticeably larger than the third main type of Roman military establishment: the fortlet (Fig. 11,c). As the name implies, this was a very small fort, usually *c.* 80–100 ft square (i.e. less than a quarter of an acre overall). The biggest single group of such sites were those attached to Hadrian's Wall

where, because of their regular spacing, at intervals of one Roman mile, they are known as milecastles (Pl. 17). This local name, however, tends to conceal the fact that they were the standard type of Roman fortlet, normally free-standing, but in this particular instance, like the Wall-forts, built into the Wall. There were 80 of them along the 80 (Roman) miles of the Wall. As with any other Roman fortification they could be turf-and-timber built or stone-built. Both types occur on the Wall, according to which section they were built in (below). On the Wall, for tactical reasons, they had two entrances, one opening through the Wall and one to the rear, but elsewhere they had only one. There is a second, associated group of fortlets, in this case free-standing, at one mile intervals, for a distance of 40 miles down the Cumbrian coast, starting from the western end of Hadrian's Wall.

Internally the buildings were fairly simple, consisting of one or two barrack blocks. The well known milecastle 48 at Poltross Burn on Hadrian's Wall contained two barracks, each *c.* 55 × 15 ft, while the early fortlet at Martinhoe (Devon) had two barracks, 60 and 55 ft long, and a small additional building. It is estimated to have housed a century (80 men), and this must be the size of garrisons for such sites, although there must have been some variation according to area or period. Martinhoe formed part of a signal-station and stood within a larger enclosure which provided space for the signal beacons. Later and more elaborate fortlets, also connected with signalling, were built along the east coast during the fourth century. There the fortlets, *c.* 100 ft square, were stone-built with corner bastions, a wide berm and an outer ditch. The interior space was dominated by the signal-tower, *c.* 50 ft square and possibly 100 ft high, and towers form the last class of Roman fortifications to be dealt with in this section.

The majority of Roman towers were much smaller than the one just mentioned.

17 Hadrian's Wall at Castle Nick milecastle, Northumberland.

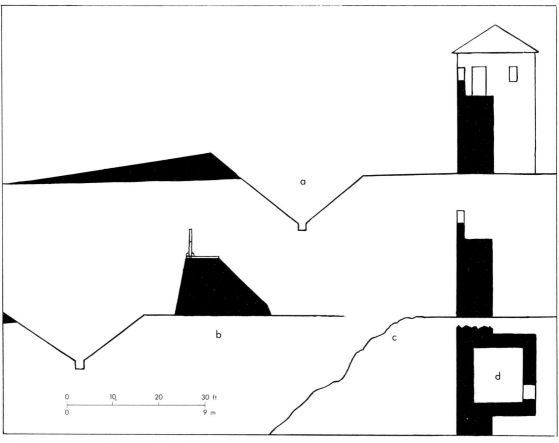

Fig. 13 Hadrian's Wall, cross-sections of: (a) stone wall, turret, ditch and glacis; (b) turf wall and ditch; (c) stone wall above crags; (d) plan of turret.

Again they figure prominently on Hadrian's Wall where they are called turrets, but they are simply standard Roman towers which were attached to the Wall, just as the auxiliary forts and milecastle fortlets were (Fig. 13, a, d). Unlike the fortlets the towers, c. 20 ft square, were always stone-built, whether they were in the stone section of the Wall or the turf-built section. Like the fortlets, they form part of the 40-mile extension down the Cumbrian coast where they are free-standing towers in the normal Roman fashion. Wooden towers, usually called signal stations, are also known, c. 10–15 ft square, standing within a surrounding earthwork which, with the ditch on the inside, was presumably more for drainage than defence.

As indicated above, such towers culminate in the very large structures built along the Yorkshire coast during the last period of Roman occupation. As well as providing an elevated platform (c. 100 ft high) for signalling purposes, the internal space, c. 30 ft square, on each of however many floors there were, must also have provided the accommodation for the garrison. In structures occupied in this way one is looking forward to the great keeps or towers which formed such an important part of medieval fortification, although the development from late Roman tower to medieval keep did not take place in the British Isles. However, these Roman towers were built also along the frontiers in Europe and probably played a significant part in the development there of the medieval keep which was introduced (and in a sense reintroduced) to these islands by the Normans in 1066.

Frontier Works

Hadrian's Wall   This, perhaps the most striking remnant of the Roman presence in Britain, is much more than a Wall, it is a whole defence system, of which the Wall is simply one, admittedly important, part. There are many other features, in front of the Wall, on the Wall and behind the Wall, all of which are an integral part of the system devised by Hadrian, Roman Emperor from AD 117–38, who instituted the building of the frontier system and who was in Britain in the early days of its construction. As far as the north and west of Britain were concerned the conquest begun in AD 43 proceeded slowly. It was not until the time of the governor Agricola, between AD 78 and AD 84, that Wales and the north of England were brought under Roman control, some forty years after the initial landings in the south-east. Agricola established a chain of forts along the Stanegate, the road from Corbridge to Carlisle, more or less where Hadrian's Wall was to be built later, and pressed on into Scotland, seemingly intent on conquering the whole country. According to his son-in-law, the Roman historian Tacitus, Agricola established a chain of forts across the Clyde-Forth isthmus, very much on the line of the later Antonine Wall. Pressing on into the Highlands he defeated the native tribes at the battle of Mons Graupius (a place not yet identified), but the result was inconclusive and Agricola was recalled to Rome before he could undertake another campaign.

During the next thirty or so years the Romans appear to have retained their hold on Lowland Scotland, with the frontier on the line of Agricolan forts between the Clyde and the Forth. There seems, however, to have been constant trouble with the native tribes in these years, in the north of England from the Brigantes, and in Lowland Scotland from the Votadini, Selgovae and Novantae, and it may have been this which brought the Emperor Hadrian himself to Britain, in AD 122. By the time of Hadrian's accession as Emperor in AD 117 the frontier appears to have been back on or near the Stanegate line, the Lowlands presumably having been abandoned a few years before.

There were two phases in the construction of Hadrian's Wall, involving a change in the basic plan while work was actually in progress. The first plan would certainly have been approved by Hadrian and its construction may already have been under way when he came to Britain in AD 122. The amended plan was probably the result of a detailed, personal examination on the spot of the terrain and of the problems facing the Roman garrison on this northern frontier. As originally conceived the system was to consist of a Wall (either in stone or turf), from Newcastle in the east to Bowness in the west (Fig. 14). At intervals of one Roman mile (1620 yd) there was to be a small fort or milecastle abutting the rear of the Wall, and between each milecastle two turrets at intervals of 540 yd. In front of the Wall was a V-shaped ditch, except where the ground was very steep and a ditch was superfluous. The garrison to man this system was to be housed in a line of forts along the Stanegate, reusing some of the original forts built by Agricola and adding new ones to the series.

The major change involved in the second plan was the abandonment of the Stanegate forts and the placing of the garrison in a new series of forts on the Wall itself, at intervals averaging about 5 miles. Thus as completed, and as it exists now, albeit in ruins, the second plan

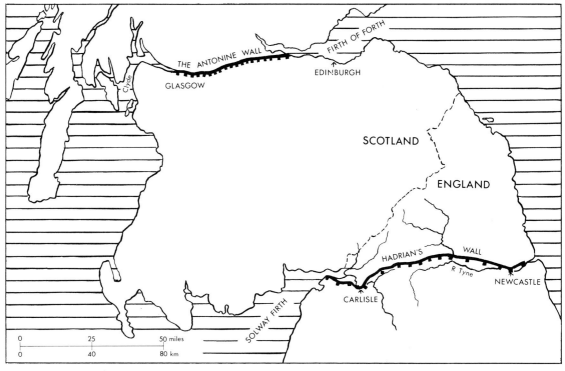

Fig. 14   Map showing the location of Hadrian's Wall and the Antonine Wall.

consisted of a Wall with a series of auxiliary forts attached to it, with fortlets or milecastles at every Roman mile in between, and with two turrets or towers between each milecastle. Other changes were involved in the second plan and these will be dealt with as parts of the system (the Wall, the milecastles, etc.) are described, together with certain other associated features, most notably the so called Vallum in the area behind the Wall.

As originally built the Wall itself was in two major sections, one built of stone, the other of turf. For about 50 (Roman) miles out of a total length of 80 (Roman) miles, it was stone-built, from Wallsend in the east to the River Irthing. The shorter western section was originally turf-built but was replaced, in two stages, by a stone wall of the same type as in the eastern sector. Starting at the eastern end there is a stone wall, 8 Roman ft ($7\frac{1}{2}$ ft) thick,

from Wallsend to Newcastle (c. 4 miles). This is known as a Narrow Wall and was an extension from Newcastle, where the wall was originally planned to start, added while other changes in plan were under way to the west. From Newcastle 45 Roman miles westwards to the River Irthing, foundations were laid for what is usually designated the Broad Wall, 10 Roman ft ($9\frac{1}{2}$ ft) thick. For about half this distance, to around milecastle 27, the Broad Wall was actually built, faced front and back with coursed masonry set in mortar and with a core of stone rubble set in puddled clay. In the remaining half of this sector the Wall was reduced to 8 Roman ft ($7\frac{1}{2}$ ft) thick (although the already-built broad foundation was retained), and the core as well as the facing was now set in mortar instead of clay (Fig. 13, a).

From the Irthing westwards to Bowness the original Wall was built of coursed turves (18 in. × 12 in. × 6 in), and was 20 ft thick and probably *c*. 12 ft high to the rampart walk. The superstructure was almost certainly of timber (Fig. 13, b). The first 5 miles of this turf rampart, from the River Irthing westwards, were replaced very quickly by a narrow stone wall, probably at the same time as the other changes mentioned above. The remaining section, from around milecastle 54 to Bowness was eventually replaced by a stone wall of intermediate width (9 Roman feet), probably *c*. AD 163. The stone wall (all sections), appears to have been 15 ft high to the rampart walk with another 6 ft or so to be added for the breastwork and crenellations.

In front of the Wall, except where rendered unnecessary by steeply sloping ground, there was normally a V-shaped ditch, which varied in dimensions from place to place but averaged overall 27 ft in width and 9 ft in depth. In a number of places the ditch had quite clearly never been completed and in one place had not even been begun. The upcast from the ditch was formed into a broad mound on its outer edge (glacis) which had the effect of increasing the effective depth by a matter of 5 or 6 ft (Fig. 13, a, b).

Built into this Wall at various intervals were three types of structure: forts, milecastles and turrets. Only the last two were part of the original plan. The inclusion of the forts was the result of the change of plan mentioned earlier while construction of the system was actually in progress.

There were originally eighty milecastles or fortlets placed, as their name indicates, at intervals of 1 Roman mile (1620 yd), along the whole length of the Wall from Wallsend to Bowness. They are numbered, for convenience, starting with no. 1 just

18   Chesters Roman fort, Hadrian's Wall: west gate and the Wall.

19 Cawfields milecastle, Hadrian's Wall.

west of Wallsend and ending at no. 80 at
Bowness. Where the Wall was turf the
milecastles too were turf-built;
correspondingly, when the Wall was
rebuilt in stone, so were the milecastles. A
milecastle is a small rectangular fort about
70 × 60 ft internally, abutting the back of
the main wall, which forms one of its sides
(Pl. 19). The other three sides were of the
same construction and dimensions as the
Wall itself. There were two gates, one
opening through the Wall and one to the
rear. The space on either side of the
central roadway was occupied by one or
two barrack buildings, each. c. 50 ft long
and 15–20 ft wide. These are generally
deemed to indicate a complement of
about 50 men for each milecastle.

Between each milecastle there were two
turrets or towers at regular intervals of
about 540 yd (Fig. 13, a, d). Unlike the
milecastles these were always stone-built,
whether they were in the stone sector of
the Wall or the turf sector. They were
about 20 ft square overall and built into
the structure of the Wall so that only
about half their area projected towards the
rear. Presumably they rose above the level
of the Wall as towers, providing lookout
points and signalling positions.

The 80-mile Wall (in stone and in turf),
the 80 milecastles and the 160 (presumed)
turrets represent the plan for the Wall as
originally conceived. The main garrison
was to be housed behind the line in a
series of auxiliary forts along the
Stanegate (the road from Corbridge to
Carlisle), making use of the forts (or some

of them) built by Agricola forty years earlier and adding new ones where required. However, even while the original plan was still being executed, it was decided to place the supporting forts on the Wall itself and this is the plan as we see it now: forts at average intervals of 5 miles; fortlets or milecastles every mile; and turrets every 540 yd, all in all a very formidable line of defences. The new plan meant sacrificing some work already completed. Excavation in a number of forts has uncovered remains of Wall, ditch, milecastles and turrets pulled down to make way for the new additions to the system. At Chesters, for example, the filled-in ditch and the foundations of the Wall and of turret 27a lie under the middle of the fort, while at Housesteads there are similar remains of the Wall (no ditch was involved

here because of the steep natural slope), and of turret 36b. The same story emerges at other forts: Carrawbrough, Great Chesters, Birdoswald and Burgh-by-Sands.

Basically the Wall forts were simply auxiliary forts of the type described earlier, and to that extent need no further description. What differentiated them from the general run of such forts was their incorporation as a group in a complex defence system and their physical link with the continuous barrier represented by the Wall. The Wall forts can be divided into two groups: those which stand astride the Wall, i.e. which project partly beyond it to the north, and those which abut the Wall, using it as their northern rampart.

Six forts projected beyond the Wall to the north (Fig. 12, a) and a seventh,

20   Chesters Roman fort, Northumberland.

Birdoswald, although now flush with the stone Wall, originally projected beyond the turf Wall, there having been a change in the line taken in this sector (from milecastles 49 to 51), when the turf Wall was rebuilt in stone. The other six forts are Wallsend at the eastern end of the line, and then (with a gap at Newcastle where the relationship to the Wall is uncertain), the next four forts in succession along the wall: Benwell, Rudchester, Halton Chesters and Chesters (Pl. 20). This means that virtually all the forts in the eastern sector, from Wallsend to just beyond the north Tyne, were of one type, generally deemed to be the accommodation for cavalry units, and indeed cavalry units are recorded at most of them, even if only for certain periods of their occupation. All the Wall forts face north, and in the case of the projecting forts they have three gateways beyond the Wall, the main gateway and the two side gateways, with the Wall running up to their southern towers. This was presumably to allow for the rapid deployment of cavalry when required. The implication of this concentration of cavalry forts is presumably that they were considered the most suitable for policing the kind of terrain that lay beyond the eastern sector of the Wall. In the western sector of the Wall Burgh-by-Sands also projects beyond the Wall and is recorded as having at one stage a cavalry unit.

Six forts are flush with the Wall, and seven if Birdoswald in its stone-Wall phase is included. These are Carrawbrough (Fig. 12, b), Housesteads, Great Chesters, Birdoswald and Stanwix, followed by a projecting fort, Burgh-by-Sands, then two more flush forts, Drumburgh and Bowness, at the western end of the Wall. Thus in broad terms the eastern forts project, the western ones are flush, the change taking place between Chesters and Carrawbrough. The flush forts show more variation than the projecting ones. Housesteads (Pl. 21) and Great Chesters, for example, being side-on to the Wall, with their long axes

running east and west and their main entrances facing east rather than north.

At varying distances behind the Wall is a feature known as the Vallum which has been a cause of endless speculation and dispute. The Vallum consists of a 20 ft wide flat-bottomed ditch with the excavated material set well back from the edges forming two banks, each about 20 ft wide, to north and south, the whole arrangement being about 120 ft wide. Opposite the Wall forts there were breaks in the banks and causeways across the ditch with gateways to control access. There have been many suggestions as to the function of the Vallum—an earlier frontier line, a customs barrier—but the most likely is that it simply demarcated a military zone immediately behind the Wall. It very carefully encloses all the Wall forts, often deliberately deviating to do so, which suggests that demarcation was its primary function. When the frontier was moved forward to the Antonine Wall the Vallum went out of use and numerous gaps in the banks and causeways across the ditch were made to facilitate traffic. At a later stage again the ditch came back into use by removing most of the causeways but not the banks, where the many gaps remained.

Between the Wall and the Vallum was a road, usually termed the military way, although this was not part of the original scheme. Presumably in the earlier phases the Stanegate, the road just south of the Wall, served for east/west communication. However, probably during or just after the major reconstruction of the system under the Emperor Septimius Severus the military way was built (the earliest milestones are dated AD 213), providing direct road communication between the Wall forts and milecastles. In most cases the road ran very close to the Wall although in those sections where the terrain was more rugged (milecastles 34–45) it deviated more often from its line to provide easier gradients for the traffic supplying the forts and milecastles.

21   Housesteads Roman fort, Northumberland.

The Antonine Wall   Under the Emperor
Antoninus Pius a new frontier system was
built further to the north, in the years AD
139–43, that is, within ten years or so of
the completion of Hadrian's Wall. It
occupied a line between the Forth and the
Clyde, only 36 miles long, the same line
chosen some sixty years before by Agricola
for the temporary frontier referred to
earlier (Fig. 14). In spite of its short
length, however, this wall brought the
whole of Lowland Scotland within the
Roman province.

The Antonine Wall was turf-built
throughout and was never replaced by a
stone wall; it had, in any case, a much
shorter life than Hadrian's Wall, being
abandoned in favour of the earlier Wall
within a generation or two of being
completed. The Antonine Wall was
narrower than the turf sector of Hadrian's
Wall, being only 14 ft wide as compared
with 20 ft but it was built upon a solid
stone foundation. The inner and outer
faces were not vertical but had a batter of
about seventy degrees. The estimated
height was about 10 ft with a 6 ft wide

rampart walk and a timber, battlemented breastwork giving an overall height of about 16 ft. In front of the wall was a ditch with a berm normally about 20 ft wide between. However, in certain places the berm was wider than this—up to 50 ft and occasionally even wider—and in one rare instance it is as much as 116 ft wide. The ditch itself is bigger than the one in front of Hadrian's Wall, normally 40 ft wide and 12 ft deep, with a square drainage channel at the bottom, although when dug through rock it is often smaller. The material excavated was thrown forward to form a mound on the outer edge of the ditch which effectively increased both its depth and its width.

In spite of its shorter length, approximately half that of Hadrian's Wall, there are more forts on the Antonine Wall, nineteen in all, giving an average of roughly one fort every two miles as compared with one in nearly five miles on Hadrian's Wall. It is quite clear that these Antonine forts were of one build with the wall and not added later as in the case of Hadrian's Wall. In fact, the sequence of work seems to have involved building the forts first and then filling in the gaps between with the wall. Like the wall the forts, with two exceptions, were turf-built, although the headquarters buildings and granaries were usually of stone, with the barrack blocks of timber. Two forts, Castlecary and Balmuidy had stone ramparts, probably because locally stone was the most abundant raw material. Outside the ramparts there were normally two or three defensive ditches. Attached to many forts were annexes, fortified in more or less the same way, which housed the civil population associated with them. The civil settlements (*vici*) associated with the forts on Hadrian's Wall, and with other forts, were normally undefended.

It has generally been assumed that the close spacing of forts on the Antonine Wall made any intermediate structure (e.g. milecastles and turrets) unnecessary.

However, there are indications, from excavation and from aerial photography, of smaller structures which appear to be similar to milecastles. If these were a regular feature then there would have been one or two milecastles between each fort as part of the completed scheme. There may also have been turrets or towers, but these, if timber-built, would be very difficult to detect in a turf wall. It has also been assumed that some of the earlier Agricolan forts were used in the new line. Claims of up to half of the wall forts have been made, and although this is not now generally accepted, it seems unlikely that the earlier Agricolan forts were completely ignored or discounted in making the new defence line. One or two at least must have their origins in Agricolan structures.

The date when the Antonine Wall was built is not in doubt, as indicated earlier. It may have been abandoned temporarily in the troubles of AD 155–8 but was certainly in use again later than that. It seems to have been abandoned finally *c.* AD 163. Thereafter Hadrian's Wall remained the effective northern frontier until the end of the Roman occupation.

Forts of the Saxon Shore

The Saxon Shore was the name used by the Romans for those parts of the south and east coasts, from the Isle of Wight around to Norfolk, where Saxon raiding was concentrated in the third and fourth centuries. To counter this threat a series of forts was built which differed from the Roman fortifications described so far. These, whether legionary or auxiliary, were nearly all first- or second-century foundations, and even when they were rebuilt in later periods, they tended to be rebuilt on the same lines. The forts along the Saxon Shore were different mainly because they were later and represented new, or at least different, ideas on fortification. They were also in a new area and had a different function.

Virtually all the earlier works were in the north and west where the greatest threat then existed, the south and east being the peaceful civil zone. In the third and fourth centuries, however, a new threat appeared in the form of Saxon raiding along the vulnerable and hitherto undefended south and east coasts, and this led to the building of the so called forts of the Saxon Shore. The use of this term has been criticized as suggesting that all the forts were built at one time as part of an integrated system. They probably were not, but this does not invalidate the use of the designation *forts of the Saxon Shore*, which simply indicates that the forts involved, whatever their particular dates of construction, were located along the stretch of coast known to the Romans as the Saxon Shore. They were designed to counter Saxon raiding and as this increased in intensity so the forts were increased to an original number probably greater than the present known total of about a dozen, plus one or two more of similar type on the west coast. There must be others of the same type still awaiting discovery.

The Saxon Shore forts are noticeably larger than auxiliary forts, varying between 4 and 10 acres in area, with an average size of about 7 acres. They also display more variation in plan. Although a number of them are rectangular and even square in plan, others are quite irregular, such as Pevensey, Sussex, which is an 8-acre oval. The walls, too, are much thicker—up to 14 ft—than auxiliary forts or legionary fortresses, and are not always backed by an earth rampart, that is, they are often free-standing walls in the manner (and dimensions) of medieval castles. In a number of cases they still stand to a considerable height, Pevensey (Sussex), 28 ft, Richborough (Kent), 25 ft, Lympne (Kent), 23 ft, and are some of the best preserved Roman remains in Britain. In most but not all cases the walls are additionally strengthened by projecting D- or U-shaped bastions, either solid or hollow, on which were mounted

the Roman *ballistae* or catapult-artillery which could be swivelled round to provide raking fire along the face of the wall. Very little is known about the internal buildings of Saxon Shore forts but these are unlikely to have differed radically from the arrangement of earlier forts.

Among the best preserved of these late Roman forts are Richborough and Lympne (Kent), Porchester (Hants), Pevensey (Sussex) and Burgh Castle (Suffolk). Richborough, built *c.* AD 290 was, as completed, 580×550 ft (*c.* 6 acres), not counting the surrounding double-ditch system which extended for about 180 ft beyond the walls on all sides (Pl. 22). Substantial portions of the northern, western and southern defences are preserved. The free-standing walls (i.e. without an earth rampart behind) are 11 ft thick and still stand over 25 ft high in places. There is a main gate with twin rectangular towers on the western side (not, incidentally, at the centre of it), and probably a matching one on the lost eastern side; on the northern and southern sides there were only small postern gates contrived in rectangular bastions, and these entrance arrangements display another difference between the Saxon Shore and earlier forts. Apart from the corner bastions which were round, the remaining bastions (one between each corner and each entrance) were rectangular. The only internal building associated with the fort was a small bath-house in the north-east corner.

Lympne is a large (*c.* 9–10 acres) and rather more irregular site. The southern, western and eastern sides are straight and at right angles to each other, consisting of a wall 14 ft thick and, in places, 23 ft high, with D-shaped bastions. The irregular northern side was bowed outwards in four straight sections with bastions at the angles between each section. Remains of the headquarters building were found in the last century, set much further back in the fort than was customary in legionary and auxiliary establishments.

22　Saxon Shore fort at Richborough, Kent.

Porchester (Hants) is almost square in plan (620 × 610 ft, *c.* 8½ acres), and is one of the best preserved of all the Saxon Shore forts, possibly because it was used in medieval times as the outer bailey of Porchester Castle, one of the castles with square keeps to be discussed in Chapter 3 (Pl. 23). This occupies the north-west corner of the Roman fort. The walls of the latter are 10 ft thick and up to 20 ft high, further strengthened by a series of twenty D-shaped bastions, including four at the corners. There were two principal entrances, east and west, deeply recessed, with twin guard chambers and single portals. The northern and southern sides contained only narrow postern gates.

Like Porchester, Pevensey in Sussex (Pl. 24) was used as the outer bailey of a medieval castle which was built in the south-eastern part of the irregularly oval enclosure (*c.* 8 acres in area). The walls are 12 ft thick and still stand, in places, 28 ft high. They are strengthened by a series of D-shaped bastions and there is a

recessed entrance with twin guard chambers at the western end.

Burgh Castle (Suffolk) is one of the smaller sites (*c.* 6 acres) and its walls are on a somewhat smaller scale than those described so far: 8 ft thick and *c.* 16 ft high, plus 4 or 5 ft for a breastwork. In plan it is a long rectangle (*c.* 650 × 300 ft) with round bastions at the rounded angles and between them and the main gateway on the eastern side.

The remaining known sites, far less well preserved or now completely gone, are as follows: Brancaster (Norfolk), Walton Castle (Suffolk), Bradwell (Essex), Reculver (Kent), Bitterne (Hants) and Carisbrooke (Isle of Wight). As mentioned earlier, there are also one or two sites of the same type and period on the western side of Britain, most notably at Cardiff Castle. This is of very much the same size and plan as Porchester, with the north-west quarter occupied by a large medieval motte with a shell-keep on top. The Roman walls, which have been restored, are $8\frac{1}{2}$ ft thick, backed by an earth rampart, and have fourteen polygonal bastions and two twin-towered gates, on the north and the south. There may have been small postern gates in the east and west walls. Much less is known about the later fort (built after AD 297) at Lancaster. The known dimensions of the north side (*c.*600 ft), and a corner bastion shown on an eighteenth-century map, suggest that the fort was similar in size and plan to Cardiff and Porchester.

Although there is considerable variation within the group of Saxon Shore forts, represented most notably by the oval site of Pevensey (Sussex), there is also some indication of regularity in such sites as Richborough, Porchester, Cardiff and possibly Lancaster. As represented by these there was a type of Saxon Shore fort with a number of clear-cut characteristics: a square or near-square plan, *c.* 500 × 600 ft; bastions at the angles and between them and the gates; two main gates on opposite sides of the fort, with two smaller, postern gates on the two remaining sides. The main variations from this standard are in size and plan, the walls, gates and bastions

being fairly regular in type. Until more examples are discovered it will not be possible to make any categorical statement about the nature of Saxon Shore forts, particularly with regard to the existence, or otherwise, of a regular type.

Town Defences

By the end of the Roman occupation all towns in Britain, large and small, were provided with defensive walls, but this was not so in the earlier part of the occupation when many towns, including London, had no defences whatsoever. Even when defences were eventually supplied they took the form of earthworks, supplemented by turf or timber, rather than stone walls, at least until *c.* AD 200. Only after that date do stone walls become the general rule and only late in the occupation, midway through the fourth century, did they receive their final structural additions, bastions similar to those encountered already in the forts of the Saxon Shore. The exceptions to this general scheme of development are the *coloniae*, the settlements for legionary veterans, which seem to have had stone

23 Saxon Shore fort and medieval castle at Porchester, Hampshire.

24   Pevensey, Sussex.

walls from a very early date. These, however, can be regarded as semi-military sites and therefore outside the circumstances governing the development of purely civilian settlements. Events in these, as far as defences are concerned, can be summarized as follows: (1) a period when settlements were undefended; (2) a period starting after the revolt led by Boudicca in AD 61 and lasting till *c.* AD 200, when the defences were of the earthwork and timber variety; (3) a period when stone-built defences were general; and (4) a period, starting in AD 343, when these stone-built defences were reorganized.

Nothing much need be said about period (1). The revolt of the Iceni under Boudicca in AD 61 found a number of important towns without defences, including London, St Albans (Verulamium) and Colchester (Camulodunum), the latter a *colonia*. The generally held view is that if such important centres as these had no defences then there were unlikely to be defences anywhere else. The destruction which resulted from the revolt seems to have initiated the second period, when earthwork defences began to be built around the developing towns. These would have been of the same general type as the defences around military establishments of the time, that is, earth ramparts revetted with turf or timber or a combination of the two. At Verulamium the ditch was 50 ft wide and 18 ft deep, with the gravel from it thrown inwards to form a rampart faced with turf, and defences like this must have become increasingly common during the

70

remainder of the first century and throughout the second.

Around the end of the second century there was a major development in the pattern of town defences. Within a very short time virtually all centres of population were provided with stone walls, and such a concentrated spell of building must have been the result of a policy decision to bring town defences up to a given level of strength, which was virtually that of military establishments. The new defences consisted of a substantial stone wall, 8–10 ft thick with an earth rampart behind and one or more ditches in front (Fig. 15, a). Where the new defences coincided with the old the existing ramparts were cut back at the front to allow the new wall to be inserted; the height of the earth rampart was generally increased at the same time. Where the town had spread beyond the earlier defences then the stone defences had to take a new, and longer line, and be built afresh from the ground up.

Some idea of the size of this undertaking can be gained from the size of some of the Roman towns as defined by their walls. London, by far the largest with an area of 330 acres, needed a total length of walling, if the river frontage is included, of over 3 miles, although most towns' requirements were less than this. Nevertheless, such places as St Albans (Verulamium), Wroxeter (Viroconium) and Cirencester (Corinium), each needed over 2 miles of walling, and many other places must have required a mile or more.

The particular circumstances which brought this considerable range of stone defences into being are not precisely known. One possibility is that they were ordered by Clodius Albinus, pretender to the Imperial throne, to secure the province while he took the legions to the continent to engage in the struggle, which he eventually lost, against the Emperor Septimius Severus; in which case, the walls would date to the years between AD 193 and 197. The other main possibility is that

they belong to the period after the same Emperor, Severus, had taken possession of the province again. When Clodius Albinus withdrew the legions the northern tribes broke through Hadrian's Wall and did considerable damage both to it and to many other military establishments in the north in AD 197. The next decade or so was occupied by the rebuilding of the Wall and all the other damaged or destroyed military bases. At the end of this period, however, there must have been a large body of workers trained in fortification work available if required. The shock caused by the northern invasion may have been sufficient for the Emperor to order, as a matter of Imperial policy, that all towns be equipped with stone walls on more or less military lines. If this is so then the stone walls of Romano-British towns date to the years around AD 210.

The last major event in the story of town defences took place nearly a century and a half later, probably in or shortly after AD 343. This involved the addition to the existing stone walls of bastions of the type encountered already in the forts of the Saxon Shore. Again, as with the stone walls, the bastions seem to have been added everywhere at more or less the same time, suggesting again a policy decision at Imperial level. Because the bastions were additions to existing defences their introduction meant in nearly every case that the whole defence system had to be reorganized (Fig. 15, b). The old ditch had to be filled in because it was too close to the wall to allow room for the projecting bastions. In any case the new defence technique demanded a different type of ditch, much wider and shallower than the earlier ditches, so that all parts of it could be commanded by the artillery (in the form of *ballistae*) mounted on the bastions. Such town wall bastions were first discovered in Caerwent (Gwent) in 1925, but they have since been uncovered at many other sites as well. They vary in shape from semi-circular (as in London), to five-sided (Caerwent) and rectangular

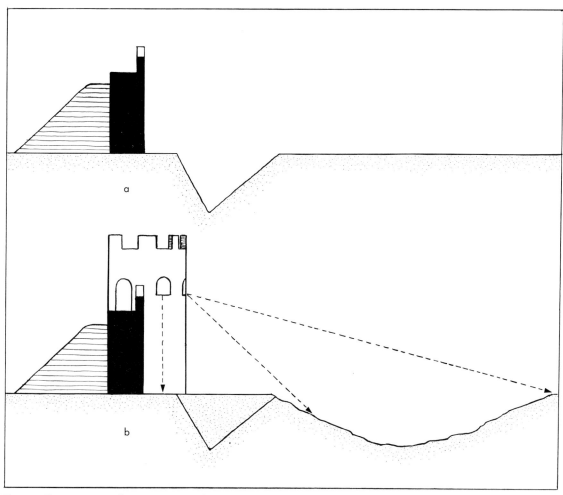

Fig. 15   Roman town walls: (a) *c.* AD 200; (b) *c.* AD 343.

(Great Casterton). There is a certain degree of irregularity in the spacing of bastions, varying from *c.* 150 to *c.* 400 ft in most cases.

What were the circumstances which produced this last major shake-up of Romano-British defences? The greatest disaster in the province was in AD 367 when the Picts, Scots and Saxons joined forces in a well co-ordinated attack which seems to have taken the authorities completely by surprise. However, it appears to have been the military bases which suffered most. There is no evidence of widespread destruction in the towns at this date, and they seem to have formed islands of refuge in an otherwise turbulent countryside. This suggests that the reorganization of their defences had already taken place and was complete by AD 367. An earlier possible date is AD 343 when the Emperor Constans visited Britain in person, in winter, an unusual time, indicating unusual conditions. There was trouble on the northern frontier; forts beyond the Wall were destroyed, and there is evidence of destruction as far south as Great Casterton (Leics.) in the midlands. The realization that invaders from north of the Wall could penetrate thus far south may have impelled Constans to order a complete reorganization of town defences on more military lines, with bastions on which to mount artillery, as in the forts of the Saxon Shore. Artillery implies professional soldiery and it looks as if there were at least small bodies of garrison troops in the towns which, with the aid of the population at large, would enable them to act as strongpoints in case of invasion. This is in keeping with the general pattern on the continent and reflects the growing defensive attitude of the third and fourth centuries in the Roman Empire as a whole. In the first two centuries confidence and aggression were the hallmarks of Roman policy along its enormous frontiers. In the third and fourth centuries, however, the ever-increasing pressure of tribes beyond these frontiers, and the economic burden of maintaining the huge military organization, forced the Romans into an increasingly more defensive attitude. Forts and fortresses were no longer springboards for attack, but strongpoints which might survive in a sea of aggression. The purely military bases were now supplemented by the towns which, equipped with walls, bastions and artillery on military lines, could be expected to survive in the same way. In this more passive role the towns, fortresses and forts look away from earlier Roman attitudes and forward to the medieval period where the castles and town walls were likewise of a primarily defensive nature.

Dark Age Fortifications

In contrast to the wide range of fortifications in the preceding Roman and succeeding medieval periods, we have comparatively little knowledge of defence works during the six centuries or so of the Dark Age period. Apart from surviving stone-built Roman works, some of which (London and Colchester, for example) are recorded as being rebuilt in the ninth century, Dark Age fortifications fall into two categories, linear earthworks and what are known as *burhs*, the origin of the modern word borough. A linear earthwork is, in most cases, a bank and ditch which instead of surrounding an area, as in the case (say) of an Iron Age hillfort, runs from point to point, marking or defending a boundary or frontier, often of considerable length. A *burh*, on the other hand, was a fortified town with earthworks or other defences surrounding it, in the manner of a Roman town, forming a stronghold in a strategic position. *Burhs* belong, in fact, to the last few centuries before the Norman Conquest of 1066, leaving only linear earthworks to fill the four centuries between AD 410 and *c*. AD 800. Both of these types will be considered in more detail below.

Linear Earthworks The most famous of these linear works is undoubtedly Offa's Dyke, built by Offa, King of Mercia (AD 757–96). By this time Mercia, originally centred on the midlands, was the dominant power in England south of the Humber and Offa, recognized in Europe as virtually king of the whole country, was in diplomatic communication with Charlemagne on more or less equal terms. The earthwork which bears his name ran from Prestatyn on the North Wales coast to Chepstow on the River Severn, a distance of some 120 miles. It consists of a bank and ditch *c*. 50 ft wide overall with the ditch on the west side, towards Wales, indicating that the builders responsible for its construction lived to the east, that is, in Mercia. Apart from modern gaps where the whole earthwork has been destroyed, the bank and ditch were not continuous anyway. In certain sections of the work, on the Severn and the Wye, the rivers were used as the line and no earthwork was built in these places.

The construction of such a work was quite clearly a very considerable undertaking and an impressive tribute to Offa's prestige and power, but was it a fortification? In the first place the work was not particularly impressive in size, but even if it had been of more formidable dimensions the question still arises: how do you defend a frontier 120 miles long? It could not possibly be continuously manned, and even if it had been, the screen of men in any one place would have been much too thin to stop a raiding band, let alone an army. There is no indication of accommodation for a supporting garrison, as on Hadrian's Wall, and the most that can be envisaged is a regular patrol along the line of the earthwork, although even that would not have prevented infiltration.

If it was not a fortification, then what was it? Virtually the only other answer possible for such a work is that it was intended to mark the frontier, very clearly, on the ground. The idea was almost certainly to leave no room for doubt in the minds of the Welsh beyond the line to the west that when they crossed this earthwork they were crossing into Mercian territory. It was a clear warning sign so that intruders could not claim that they had wandered in by mistake. Once they crossed the boundary mark they were risking retribution from the most powerful monarch of his day. The concept of Offa's Dyke is the concept of a strong sovereign. A weaker king could not have built such a frontier, still less could he have enforced its clear warning.

More or less parallel to, and to the east of the northern part of Offa's Dyke, is another of the same type, Wat's Dyke. This runs from the Dee estuary to a little south of Oswestry, a distance of c. 35 miles, usually some 2–3 miles to the east of the longer work. Wat's Dyke faces in the same direction as Offa's Dyke and presumably was intended to perform the same function, but at an earlier date. Wat was apparently a predecessor of Offa and it may have been from Wat's (apparently unfinished) frontier that Offa inherited the idea of a continuous frontier mark in the form of a bank and ditch.

In the south of England generally similar earthworks seem to belong to an earlier period, towards the end of the sixth century, and to have performed a similar function in marking a frontier. Wansdyke runs from the county of Avon, just south of Bristol, to north-west Hampshire, in a generally east/west line, with the ditch on the north side. Wansdyke exists in two main sections with a 10 mile gap between, the presumption being that this part has been destroyed. There is, however, no evidence that an earthwork in this section ever existed and the two parts of the Wansdyke may be two separate works. The eastern section, along the Marlborough Downs, is, in fact, of more massive construction than the western one, and is generally attributed to Ceawlin, King of the West Saxons, as the mark of his northern frontier in the last years of the sixth century. The western section could well be of the same general period and purpose without necessarily forming part of the same work.

Other notable linear works, presumably of similar date, include Bokerly Dyke, on the Dorset/Hampshire border, and the Devil's Dyke, Cambridgeshire, some 9 miles long and, where best preserved (near Swaffham Prior), still of formidable dimensions.

Burhs   There is no doubt that the second category of Dark Age works, the *burhs* or defended towns, are fortifications in the true sense of the word and not simply boundary marks. Apart from the surviving earthworks (below), there are written records that many more were built. Many of these, however, were in places subsequently reused or afterwards continuously occupied, and the remains of the original *burh* must be buried deep beneath later castles and present-day towns. Presumably, however, the surviving examples are a more or less representative sample of what formerly existed in this category.

The establishment of a system of *burhs*

or fortified towns was begun by Alfred the Great (AD 849–99), and these were the only fortifications which existed in England before the Norman Conquest. The English certainly had no castles, as so often stated, but they were not entirely defenceless. Probably the best surviving examples of Anglo-Saxon *burhs* are Wareham (Dorset) and Wallingford (formerly Berks., now Oxon.), which are broadly similar in size and plan and may represent a standard type.

Wareham is situated between two rivers, the Piddle to the north and the Frome to the south, which are so close to the defences on these sides that they are almost outer moats. The site is more or less rectangular in plan and measures *c.* 2300 × 2000 ft; the main variation in shape is on the south where the defences follow the curving line of the river. The well-preserved remains consist of a substantial bank and ditch, *c.* 110 ft wide overall. The bank rises up to 15 ft above the interior and falls as much as 25 ft to the bottom of the outer ditch. Excavation has established that there were two structural phases. As first built the rampart, wedge-shaped in cross-section, was about 10 ft high with a timber facing or revetment at the front. Subsequently the height of the rampart was increased by at least 5 ft and the timber facing was replaced by a stone wall. Later again, after the conquest, a timber motte-and-bailey was built in the south-west corner of the enclosure.

Wallingford is of very similar dimensions (*c.* 2500 × 1800 ft) and makes use of the Thames on its eastern side; it too is sub-rectangular in plan. Its surviving banks rise about 10 ft above the interior and fall some 20 ft to the ditch bottom which is 5 ft below external ground level, that is, only marginally smaller than those of Wareham in its second phase, and probably of the same size in its first phase. To complete the parallel, a timber motte-and-bailey castle was added in the north-east corner of the enclosure in the post-conquest period.

Another earthwork can be included with Wareham and Wallingford as almost certainly an Anglo-Saxon *burh*. Cricklade in north Wiltshire is again roughly rectangular in plan and *c.* 1350 ft square, somewhat smaller than the other two. There is evidence that the rampart had a front face of stone, similar to the second phase at Wareham.

The evidence of these three sites makes it feasible to suggest that there was a regular type of Anglo-Saxon *burh* which was rectangular or near-rectangular in plan and from 50–100 acres in area. The rectangular plan may be an inheritance or memory of Roman practice, or a copy based on surviving Roman examples, however patched up; it may even, in some cases, be the result of following the line of earlier Roman defences on the same site. Area and dimensions are an indication of the amount of work involved in building such fortifications. A site enclosing 100 acres would call for defences totalling over 8000 ft in overall length. Wareham and Wallingford are unlikely to have been the only sites of such size in England, and this assumption goes some way towards filling the picture of Dark Age fortification which, although never on the massive scale of the later medieval period, was by no means insignificant, particularly in its last couple of centuries.

Burhs specially built, such as Wareham and Wallingford, and Roman defences rebuilt, such as London and Colchester, form two groups of Dark Age fortifications, leaving linear earthworks to one side as boundary or frontier marks. A third group is formed by the reuse of fortifications even earlier than Roman, that is, from the preceding Iron Age period. There is at least one well-documented and surviving example of an Iron Age fort which was rebuilt in the tenth century by Aethelfleda, daughter of Alfred the Great. The site is Eddisbury in Cheshire which, at the end of the Iron Age period, had two ramparts and two ditches surrounding a roughly oval area of about 12 acres. The site was rendered useless by the Romans and remained unfortified until late in the Dark Ages when, as part of a programme of making Mercia secure by means of a series of strongpoints, Aethelfleda, the 'Lady of the Mercians', established a number of *burhs* in her territory, including Eddisbury, in the years AD 912–18. The new ramparts were built directly over the collapsed Iron Age remains and the old ditches were re-excavated. The result is that what is now visible at Eddisbury is not Iron Age at all but Dark Age, even though the Iron Age remains, had they not been built on, would have looked very much the same. No doubt one or two other hillforts were similarly adapted to the needs and conditions of the late Anglo-Saxon period.

Although strictly speaking the Dark Age (AD 410–1066) forms the earliest part of the medieval period, its fortifications, such as they are, are more appropriately considered in the context of Roman, and indeed earlier, works. On the whole, Anglo-Saxon fortifications look back rather than forward, utilizing earlier structures or, where building anew, doing so on lines which recall Roman practice. It is for this reason that the succeeding Norman fortifications provide such a striking contrast to what had gone before, and why they very properly mark the beginning of a new chapter.

3 Castles with Keeps

'Next to the Briton the Norman has left the most enduring, the most numerous, and the most impressive marks upon our soil. He was as great a sapper as the Celt, as systematic and methodical as was the Roman.' These remarks, from Hadrian Allcroft's classic book, *Earthwork of England* (1908, pp. 401–2), reflect the very great changes in fortification following the Norman Conquest of England in 1066. The Normans brought with them an entirely new tradition of fortification, quite unlike anything that had gone before— prehistoric, Roman or Anglo-Saxon. The new types introduced then began the great period of medieval castle building which was to last until the advent of artillery, and the very different forms of defence work which it called for, some five centuries later.

The vast majority of Norman castles are of a type known as motte-and-bailey, a term which refers to their layout or plan (Fig. 16). They consist of two main parts, a *motte* or conical mound of earth, surmounted by a tower or keep, built of timber or stone, and a *bailey*, an attached outer enclosure at a lower level, defended by an earth-and-timber or stone wall. In a few cases the place of the motte is taken by an inner enclosure or ringwork (presumably containing the keep), of the same type as, and at the same level as, the bailey, and the terms inner bailey and

outer bailey are appropriate. Such castles can be designated ringwork-and-bailey. The main group of castles without mottes, however, are those with large stone keeps, most of which were built on level ground for structural reasons. These likewise had a bailey, defended by a stone wall, although later developments have often obscured these early arrangements. Thus all three arrangements are essentially the same: motte-and-bailey, in which the motte supports the keep, ringwork-and-bailey in which the ringwork contains the keep, and (stone) keep-and-bailey where the keep stands without a motte.

Not unexpectedly, remains of many of the stone castles have survived, some of them incorporated in more elaborate works of later centuries. But stone castles, even if they were in use for longer periods, were always in a minority as compared with timber-built castles. Unfortunately there are no visible remains of timber-built castles in the British Isles. What do survive, of course, are the earthworks of which the timber structures formed part: the motte which supported the timber keep and the bailey which contained the ancillary buildings. Where there is no visible or recorded evidence of stonework it is generally presumed that the work in question was timber-built, and while stone-built castles are numbered in their hundreds, motte-and-bailey earthworks without evidence of stone buildings (i.e. presumably timber-built) are numbered in their thousands and occupy a significant place in the British landscape.

The Motte

The motte of a Norman castle is a flat-topped conical mound which can vary considerably in size. Many such mounds are of quite modest dimensions, perhaps 20 ft high above the bottom of the ditch surrounding them, 80–90 ft in diameter at the base and 25–30 ft across the top although, allowing for erosion, the latter dimensions might originally have been 35–40 ft. The motte at Abinger (Surrey), one of the few excavated examples, is very much of this size, and its timber arrangements (below, p. 81), are probably typical of a large number of motte-and-bailey castles. Of very different dimensions is the motte at Thetford (Norfolk) which is 80 ft high, 80 ft in diameter at the summit, and 360 ft in diameter at the base. In fact, not many mottes are of this height, although quite a few are much greater in area. Many of the stone-built shell-keeps (below, p. 102) stand on mottes with summits ranging in size from about 80 ft to about 120 ft in diameter. The vast majority of mottes are to be found in the size range from Abinger (35–40 ft) to Thetford (80 ft), as far as their summit diameters are concerned. At the other end of the scale, however, there are mottes with even larger summits, up to 300 ft in diameter, and these inevitably raise the question of the composition and structure of such earthworks.

Although many mottes, particularly those on level ground, must be completely artificial, the Normans were no less willing than the Celts to take advantage of natural features when these presented themselves. If there was a suitable hill in the area this would be adapted to their needs by scarping, that is, steepening the sides by cutting away the lower slopes so as to leave the shape of a motte. Such a

motte is entirely natural and the existence of this practice may account for some, if not all, of the very large mottes mentioned earlier. It would have been an enormous undertaking, for example, to build mottes with summits the size of Old Sarum (Wilts., diameter, 300 ft; Pl. 4), Framlingham (Suffolk, 300 × 200 ft, oval), Clun (Salop, 170 × 130 ft, oval) or Knepp (Sussex, 220 × 140 ft, oval). Mottes of this size were probably only feasible where natural conditions were suitable. In all of these cases it looks as if the terrain was such that a very wide (even if relatively low) motte could be produced by scarping the sides of an existing hill. The result is a motte which is much larger than required simply to support a square keep, or even a shell-keep; it forms, in fact, an enclosure rivalling the bailey in size. Indeed, the term inner bailey is used at Old Sarum for the motte. There, the outer bailey is a former Iron Age hillfort, the domed interior of which seems to have been levelled when the castle was built, except for the centre, which was left at its original height to form the motte or inner bailey. Where an inner enclosure of comparable size was required on level ground it was probably easier to provide it by enclosing the space required with a bank and a ditch rather than by building an enormous artificial motte, and this may explain the existence of sites where the place of the motte is taken by a ringwork (below, p. 80).

So far nothing has been said about the composition and structure of those mottes, large or small, which were entirely or partly artificial. Part of the material for the motte must have been derived from the ditch which surrounded it, but in most cases additional material would have been required to bring the motte up to any appreciable size. But wherever the material was derived from, it is quite clear that the motte was something more than a simple dump of earth. If it had been no more than that it would have been a very suspect support for even the simplest of timber towers, and would, in addition, have been dangerously prone to erosion. The Bayeux tapestry which, among other things, illustrates the motte-and-bailey castles at Dol, Rennes, Dinan and Bayeux in France and Hastings in England, gives some indication of the structure of the motte at Hastings which can be seen to be composed of alternating horizontal layers of material. Although the evidence is somewhat fragmentary, it is clear from various sites that the layers used included stone, clay, peat, chalk rubble and earth, the latter probably rammed or beaten

down to provide greater stability. What is important is not so much the particular material as the way the materials were used. A motte composed of alternating layers of stone and beaten earth, for example (one of the more likely combinations), would have provided a very adequate support for a timber keep, and other materials used in the same way would have produced a similar result. A final thick coating of clay over the whole motte, evidence for which has been found, would have guarded against erosion of the sides and, in wet conditions, would have made the scaling of the slope virtually impossible.

Fig. 16 Reconstruction and section of a timber motte-and-bailey castle.

Although mottes have been described as either natural (i.e. produced by scarping), or artificial (built in the way just described), it is probable that there is a third, fairly large, group which falls somewhere between the two, in which the lower part of the motte is natural but the upper part is artificial (Fig. 16). The ratio of the three groups to each other is a matter of guesswork. The fact is that we know very little about the internal construction of medieval mottes. In the same connection it has been suggested that, instead of simply sitting on top of the motte, some keeps were carried down through the motte to the original ground surface. This can only apply to keeps on artificial mottes (whether partly or wholly artificial) and will be further considered in the section on keeps.

The normal concomitant of a motte is a bailey (below), but there are a number of castles which consist of a motte with its surrounding ditch and nothing else, although in some cases the absence of a bailey may be explained by ploughing or other destructive agencies. In addition to these, however, there are a number of mottes which never had baileys. These may have been outposts from some larger castle where the ancillary buildings of the bailey were not required, or they may represent more temporary fortifications, built for local advantage during the civil war in King Stephen's reign (1135-54), or during a much longer period, on the Welsh frontier where castles changed hands frequently in a long drawn out, see-saw struggle. In neither case, again, would there be much interest in a bailey and the sort of buildings it normally contained. As can be imagined, the mottes for such castles were frequently quite small, of the dimensions given earlier. There are, however, a few larger examples. The motte at Clifford's Hill (Northants.) is of similar dimensions to the one mentioned earlier at Thetford (Norfolk, p. 78), with a diameter at the summit of some 80 ft. In this case the explanation may be that all the buildings needed could be accommodated on the motte, thus eliminating the need for an additional enclosure of the bailey type.

Ringworks

Before dealing with baileys and other ancillary enclosures, something must be said about those inner enclosures which in some cases take the place of the motte as the central feature of the castle. Ringworks at Buckenham (Norfolk) and Saltwood (Kent) are of comparable size with Old Sarum and Framlingham and may be simply an alternative method of providing similarly large inner enclosures where a natural motte was not possible and where an entirely man-made one was too big an undertaking.

The Bailey

As the name motte-and-bailey suggests, most mottes were accompanied by an outer enclosure or bailey; in some cases there is more than one bailey, and in still other cases there are additional linked enclosures of a much larger size taking in a complete village or town. The simplest type of bailey is a D- or U-shaped enclosure on one side of the motte, the two together forming a figure of eight or simply an oval shape. The bailey is surrounded by a ditch which is linked on to the one surrounding the motte, so that there is a complete circuit of ditch around the whole site, together with an isolating ditch between the two separate parts. The material from the bailey ditch was thrown inwards to form a rampart, almost certainly surmounted or revetted by timberwork. Although many baileys are no greater in overall diameter than the mottes they accompany, the bailey can, in fact, be of virtually any size. At Berkhamsted, for example, the bailey is *c.* 400 × 300 ft, and there are baileys of broadly similar dimensions at Lewes, Lincoln and Carisbrooke. The west bailey at Windsor is larger again, *c.* 550 × 400 ft.

There are, in fact, two baileys at Windsor and other sites with two, and in some cases more, baileys are by no means uncommon. At Windsor the second (upper) bailey (*c.* 400 × 350 ft) is on the opposite side of the motte from the first and therefore completely isolated from it. There is a similar arrangement at Arundel (Sussex), on a slightly smaller scale, and also at Castle Rising (Norfolk), although there the central structure is a ringwork and not a motte. In most cases, however, the baileys are adjacent to each other, either side by side, both impinging on the motte ditch, or in line, one next to the motte and one beyond. An example of the first type is provided by Nether Stowey (Somerset), where a broad (160 ft diameter), relatively low motte has two such adjacent baileys, and an example of the second by Brinklow (War.) where a much taller motte (top diameter 35 ft), has two triangular baileys arranged in line. Where there are more than two baileys then both side-by-side and in-line arrangements may be involved. In some cases the baileys completely surround the motte, as at Pickering (Yorks.), and Old Sarum (Wilts.), although the latter is the result of placing the motte inside a large, pre-existing earthwork (an Iron Age hillfort) and then subdividing it radially into a series of baileys. Note should also be taken of those cases where the motte stands in the middle of the bailey, rather than on one side of it, as at Barwick-in-Elmet (Yorks.), and Bramber (Sussex). The number, size and arrangement of baileys is infinitely variable and, as can be imagined, no two sites are exactly alike.

In addition to baileys there are in some cases additional, much larger earthworks which are termed village enclosures, precursors of the later walled towns of the period. Castle Acre (Norfolk) is a fairly ordinary motte-and-bailey castle with a shell-keep on the motte; linked to it on the south-west, however, is a larger rectangular area (*c.* 800 × 600 ft),

surrounded by a bank and ditch which, in fact, formed the defence works of a village associated with the castle. There are similar enclosures at Framlingham (Suffolk), Meppershall (Beds.), Ongar and Pleshey (Essex) and Rhuddlan (Clwyd). The pattern of a castle with a linked town wall will be encountered again in much more elaborate stone-built form in a later section, most particularly at Conway and Caernarvon in North Wales (below, pp.134–6).

Timber Castles

The earthworks just described (motte, ringwork, bailey, village enclosure) were, however, only part of the fortification picture. As indicated earlier, a very large number of them (possibly around 2000 or so) were completed with timberwork which has left no trace on the surface; nor is there very much evidence from below the surface since very little excavation has been carried out in motte-and-bailey earthworks, except those with fairly obvious stone remains. Where there is no surface evidence of stone then the presumption is that the structures associated with the surviving earthworks were built of timber. For the form these timber structures took we have to rely on certain written accounts, on the excavated motte at Abinger (Surrey), mentioned earlier, and on the Bayeux tapestry which, in addition to illustrating the structure of a motte (above, p. 78), also shows what went on top in the shape of timber building.

Although many of the details are lacking, the nature of the timber works in motte-and-bailey castles is known, if only in broad terms. The space on top of the motte was occupied by a rectangular timber building, almost certainly two or three storeys (possible more) high, in other words, a tower or keep on the same lines as the stone keeps to be considered later. The timber keep was surrounded by an open space varying in width according to the size of the building and the area of the motte. At the edge of the motte was a timber palisade or rampart, possibly 8 or 10 ft high, with a rampart walk for the defenders some 4 or 5 ft above the interior.

The excavated motte at Abinger (Surrey), mentioned earlier, followed this pattern and was probably typical of the vast majority of timber-built motte-and-bailey castles. The Abinger motte was c. 35–40 ft in diameter at the top. Approximately in the centre were the post-holes for the timber uprights of the tower. Some twenty post-holes (representing the original building of c. 1100 and a later, twelfth-century reconstruction), formed a square roughly 12 ft × 12 ft, indicating clearly the very limited dimensions of the plan. Even allowing for several floors above, the total amount of accommodation thus provided could never have been very great; the question of size will be considered further below. About 8–10 ft beyond the tower was a ring (c. 33 ft in diameter) of closely set post-holes (c. 50 in number), to house the timbers of the palisade around the summit of the motte. About 3 ft inside the ring was another, more widely spaced (c. 25 post-holes), which housed either reinforcing struts or the uprights for a rampart walk for the defenders. A gap some 5 ft wide between two large post-holes in the outer ring indicates the position of the entrance.

The arrangements at Abinger were probably typical of a very large number of motte-and-bailey castles. Many mottes are of similar size and probably originally supported timber towers of at least the same dimensions as the one at Abinger. It is unlikely that they were ever much smaller than this (c. 12 ft square), and the probability is that Abinger was at the lower end of the size scale. In the absence of any coherent body of excavation evidence it is difficult to make any precise statement but possibly dimensions of 20 ft × 20 ft or thereabouts would represent the average size of timber keeps in motte-and-bailey castles. This average would embrace smaller keeps, such as Abinger, and presumably also make allowance for some larger keeps, possibly up to 25 or even 30 ft square, providing, on the several floors, very adequate amounts of accommodation.

The total amount of accommodation would, of course, vary with the number of floors and this again is a matter for speculation. We know from written accounts that there were at least two floors above the ground floor level and it is possible that there were, in some cases, three. It is unlikely, however, that there were, except in rare instances, more than three. Whatever the number of floors it is almost certain that the tower was topped off with a pitched or sloping roof; the English climate would make any other form very impractical. The actual housing accommodation would be on the first floor and above. The ground floor, at the level of the motte surface, would probably have been used for storage, although it has been suggested that these timber towers were stilted, in other words that the ground floor level was open except for the main uprights, so as to allow more room on the summit. This could well have been so in the smaller castles but is perhaps less likely where the motte provided adequate space for both tower and circulation. In the same connection it has also been suggested that these main supporting timbers rose, not from the top of the motte, but from the original ground surface below the motte. In other words the timber tower was built first, on tall stilts, and the motte was then piled around it, possibly as a protection against fire. This clearly did not happen at Abinger, and probably not at a great many other sites either, but could well have been used where speed was important and there was insufficient time to construct a solid motte in the way described earlier. The stilts or legs would give the tower stability while the mantle of earth, the motte, would guard against undermining or fire.

Fire must also have been a hazard to

the tower as a whole, both from internal domestic sources at all times, and from external, hostile sources in time of war. A tower three or four storeys high with large expanses of timber surface was obviously very vulnerable to attack by fire, and there is some evidence that timber keeps were given a cladding of shields or skins to prevent this. Such cladding was probably not a permanent feature and in times of peace the tower would have presented a rather different appearance. Just what this appearance was is again a matter for speculation but it is very unlikely that there was not some attempt at decoration in the form of painting and carving. Even if a plain, purely utilitarian tower was built, the climate in Britain is such that painting is virtually essential, for preservation if not for decoration. Since these towers were homes as well as fortifications, considerations of beauty, pride and prestige would be involved and it would be the most natural thing in the world to try to beautify as well as preserve. Similarly with carved decoration, which is an almost natural extension of timber construction. In an entirely timber building the possibilities for carved decoration are almost endless and it seems unlikely that advantage was not taken of these in the building of timber motte-and-bailey castles. Although some keeps may have been fairly plain, unadorned timber towers, it is difficult to imagine that there were not others, perhaps many others, in which painting and sculpture had been used to considerable effect. The timber keeps shown on the Bayeux tapestry may not be due entirely to the imagination of the embroiderer. They may reflect, at least in part, the normal practice of embellishing such structures with painting and carving.

The remaining features of timber motte-and-bailey castles can be dealt with fairly briefly. Access to the motte from the bailey was by means of a removable timber bridge across the ditch and, where required, a flight of steps up the slope of the motte to the gateway in the palisade on the summit. Where the motte was relatively low a sloping bridge with a removable section would probably have been sufficient, but on a large motte the angle for a bridge alone would have been too steep and a flight of steps would have been needed as well. The bailey would have been defended by a bank of earth, thrown inwards from the surrounding ditch, surmounted or revetted by a timber fence. Within the bailey would have been additional timber buildings for the followers, retainers and servants of the owner of the castle and for stables, granaries and so forth. Additional baileys would have been defended in the same way as also, presumably, would the village enclosures attached to some motte-and-bailey castles described earlier.

In spite of the apparently large number of stone castles which have survived there is no doubt that the commonest type of Norman fortifications were the timber-built motte-and-bailey castles, several thousand of which must have been built during the century and a half following the Norman Conquest in 1066. In terms of distribution their surviving earthworks are spread widely over England and Wales, lowland and eastern Scotland (the Highlands are virtually blank) and the eastern half of Ireland. Not all of these were built at the same time, nor for the same reasons; nor is the distribution even from area to area. A very large number of motte-and-bailey timber castles must have been built in the early days of the conquest when Norman lords were establishing themselves in alien and hostile territory. There was another outburst of building during the civil wars (the Anarchy) in Stephen's reign (1135–54), when timber castles were erected as temporary expedients, only to be abandoned when order was re-established. The wide spread of motte-and-bailey earthworks in the eastern half of Ireland was a result of the invasion of the country in 1167, the pattern following that of England a century or so earlier. By far the densest concentration of timber castles was in the borderlands between England and Wales, where earthwork remains of several hundred such castles reflect the long struggle put up by the Welsh against the Norman and later English would-be conquerors. Many of the more permanent timber castles were rebuilt at a later stage in stone, to add to the range of stone castles already in existence, for even in the earliest days of the conquest the Normans were by no means confined to timber-built motte-and-bailey works. Rather than a single type they brought with them a comprehensive range of fortification techniques which they used as need and material dictated in each particular case.

Stone Castles

The more durable equivalent of the timber tower is the rectangular stone keep which is pre-eminently the structure associated with the Norman fortification. Remains of such keeps, often incorporated in later buildings, are considerable, but they by no means represent the full range of Norman stone castles. Apart from round and polygonal keeps, there are also what are known as shell-keeps, which survive in not inconsiderable numbers. All of these types will be considered in turn.

Although many of them belong to the twelfth century and later, the building of stone castles in Britain began within a dozen or so years after 1066. The stone keep already existed in Normandy and elsewhere on the continent, so that there was no question of it developing here from the wooden prototype. That stage of development, if ever there was one, had long since taken place elsewhere. The choice between a timber castle and one of stone depended on the conditions obtaining in a particular place at a particular time. Where speed was essential then a timber structure would be erected, perhaps to be replaced at a later stage, often during the twelfth century, by one of stone. Where time allowed, and other

conditions made it desirable, a stone castle would be erected from the beginning. There was no hard and fast rule; the Normans made use of whatever type was indicated by particular conditions.

Stone keeps vary considerably in size, from very large examples such as Colchester (Essex), c. 150 × 150 ft in area, to very small ones such as Clitheroe (Lancs.), only c. 32 ft square externally and c. 16 ft square inside. Stone keeps usually stood on a splayed-out plinth or foundation which not only provided very solid support for the building above but also made undermining by attackers very difficult. Access to the keep was normally at first (sometimes second) floor level by means of a stone staircase, housed in a structure built against the side of the keep and known as a forebuilding. The outer walls of the keep were reinforced with flat pilasters and the corners of the building were carried up in four turrets above the level of the parapet. The main part of the walls also rose well above the (wooden) roof level of the top storey, to protect it from attack by fire. Most rectangular stone keeps possess some if not all of these features, as will emerge from the account to follow.

Probably the best known of all the great stone keeps is the White Tower of the Tower of London (Pl. 25). As originally built (c. 1078), the castle consisted of the keep and a bailey running down to the Thames in the south-east angle of the Roman city wall. It is now incorporated as the central feature of a much larger castle, the whole of which we call the Tower of London, but the original Tower was the great square keep built by William the Conqueror as a fortress, palace and seat of government. In plan, the White Tower is rectangular, c. 120 × 96 ft (not counting the north-east corner tower and the semi-circular apse at the south-east), with walls some 12–14 ft thick. The whole structure stands on a high, sloping plinth or base and is 90 ft high to the top of the main structure, with the

25   The Tower of London.

corner turrets rising still higher. As built, the White Tower had three storeys, basement, entrance level and main floor. Entry to the middle storey was by means of a forebuilding now entirely gone, and the corresponding doorway is blocked up. The basement was reached by a spiral staircase in the north-east corner turret and this, and other turret staircases, also gave access to the upper floor and the battlements.

The plan of the building is virtually the same on all three floors and is dictated by the presence of a chapel and its crypt, and by a cross wall, a normal feature in large keeps, in order to reduce the span for flooring purposes. The basement, which was, in fact, above ground level and rose above the plinth, consisted of three main parts, a large room (*c.* 90 × 37 ft), to the west of the cross wall, a smaller room (*c.* 61 × 26 ft) to the east of it, and the sub-crypt of the chapel. The two floors above follow the same plan. The middle (entrance) storey has two rooms of very much the same size as the ones below,

together with the crypt of the chapel on the floor above. Externally this storey is represented by the lowermost of the three rows of windows in the White Tower. The third (main) storey is represented by the two remaining (upper) rows of windows, for reasons which will be explained below.

The third storey provides the principal rooms of the castle. To the west of the cross wall is the great hall (96 × 40 ft), to the east of it the great chamber (65 × 28 ft), together with the chapel with its apsidal or semi-circular east end. This storey was of much greater height than the ones below and had a gallery 16 ft above floor level running around the outer walls and connected to the triforium or gallery above the aisles of the chapel. This gallery has its own row of windows (the top row externally), in addition to the (middle) row which served the lower part of the great hall, the great chamber and the chapel, and this is why the third storey is represented on the exterior by the two top rows of windows. At a later stage an additional storey was created by inserting a floor at gallery level, but this was not part of the original plan.

The basic simplicity of the plan makes it difficult to appreciate just how much accommodation the White Tower provided, even before the insertion of the additional floor. Not counting the chapel or the galleries, the total floor area of the three storeys was something over 16,000 square ft. This, however, was a royal establishment, with many functions to cope with, and the eventual insertion of an extra floor indicates that even 16,000 square ft was not enough. In terms of function the basement was probably used for storage, particularly of food, large reserves of which would be needed in the event of a prolonged siege. The second, entrance storey, was probably given over to the accommodation of the garrison and servants while the third storey contained the Royal apartments, the great hall where the king, ministers and courtiers dined, were entertained and spent much of their day. The great chamber was a more private room where the king could carry on the business of government with particular ministers and also have his personal apartments. Although only solid main walls now survive it has to be remembered that these very large rooms were probably subdivided into smaller and more convenient units by means of lighter timber walls and screens, so that the original layout was probably much more complex than now appears.

During the following two centuries many additions were made to the original keep and inner bailey, particularly under Henry III (1216–72), and Edward I (1272–1307), transforming the structure into what we know today as the Tower of London. The final result was a concentric arrangement of keep, inner bailey (now gone), middle bailey and outer bailey, broadly similar to the eventual arrangement at Dover Castle (below, p. 86).

The great keep at Colchester (Essex) was built about the same time as the White Tower, c. 1080, and closely resembles it in plan. Although larger in area than the latter (c. 153 × 115 ft, not counting the corner turrets), its remains are rather less impressive, mainly because it appears to be unfinished, the two storeys which remain being all that were ever built. There is no doubt that it was originally intended to be a three storey structure with the same arrangement as the Tower, basement, entrance floor and main floor, with great hall, great chamber and chapel. If these rooms were to have been of similar height to those of the Tower, perhaps with mural galleries, then externally Colchester needs to be envisaged as about twice its present height, with the corner turrets higher again.

The White Tower and Colchester are only two, admittedly outstanding, examples of stone keeps built during the next century or so. Few were quite as large as these, but one or two are equally impressive. The keep at Dover, now the central feature of a whole complex of fortifications, belongs to the end of the period and was built by Henry II (1154–89). Excluding the elaborate forebuilding, the keep is virtually a cube in shape, 98 × 96 ft in plan, and 95 ft high (Pl. 26). Its walls are unusually thick (varying from 17 to 21 ft), and this may explain the unusual number of mural chambers in the upper levels in addition to the principal rooms. The floor arrangements are similar to those of the Tower (basement, middle storey, main floor with mural gallery). However, in this case, entry was at main storey rather than middle storey level (Fig. 17). The elaborate forebuilding carried the entrance steps along the eastern side of the keep, around the angle and across most of the northern side, ending at main floor level, with access down to the two storeys below by means of spiral staircases. The four principal rooms on the second and third storeys are c. 50 × 20 ft in area, but there are another twenty or so rooms of more modest dimensions (c. 15 × 10 ft or

26   Dover Castle, Kent.

Fig. 17   The keep, Dover Castle: plan of second and third storeys.

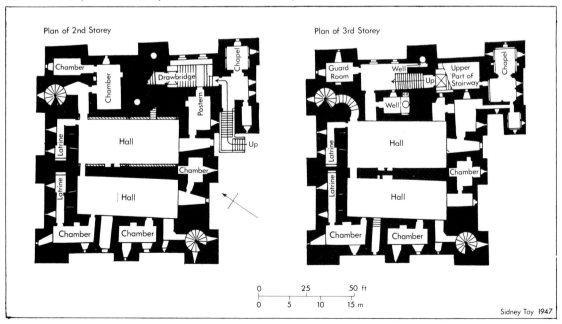

thereabouts) contrived in the great thickness of the walls. The curtain wall of the inner bailey with its square towers and entrance barbican was also built at this period, as was, probably, part of the curtain wall on the eastern side of the middle bailey. During the next three-quarters of a century, mostly under King John (1199–1216) and Henry III (1216–72), much additional work was done on the outer defences of the castle and by about 1256 Dover Castle had reached its present day extent and appearance. The completion of the middle bailey during this period had, in effect, produced a concentric castle (keep standing in inner bailey, inside middle bailey), as at the Tower of London, and both of these works look forward to the great Edwardian concentric castles of North Wales and elsewhere (below, pp. 108–15).

Among the remaining large, well-preserved keeps are Newcastle-on-Tyne,

27 The forebuilding of the keep at Newcastle.

Rochester and Norwich. Newcastle, of similar date to Dover, likewise has a large number of mural chambers contrived in thick walls (c. 15 ft thick), and entry via a forebuilding, at third storey level (Pl. 27). The available internal space at each floor level is only c. 27 × 21 ft, the rest of the plan being accounted for by walls. The keep stood originally within a triangular bailey, the walls of which are now mostly gone, except for portions on the south and east. Rochester (Kent), in its stark simplicity, is in many ways one of the most impressive of all the great Norman keeps (Pl. 28). Preserved to the top of its corner turrets it rises to a height of over 120 ft, the tallest of all the stone keeps in the British Isles. It has four storeys, with a great forebuilding giving entry at second storey level. A cross wall divides the interior into two main rooms, each c. 40 × 20 ft, on each of the four storeys, with a mural gallery around the walls of the third storey, where the main hall is situated. Norwich (c. 100 ft square) is noted chiefly for the architectural decoration of its exterior, most of which is a refacing of 1834–9, although faithfully following the well-recorded original appearance. It stands high above the town on a motte which must be largely if not entirely natural. There are other great rectangular keeps at Bamburgh and Norham (Northumb.) (Pls 29 and 30), Bowes (Durham), Canterbury (Kent), Corfe (Dorset) (Pl. 31), Driffield (Derby., foundations only), Kenilworth (War.) (Pl. 32), Middleham (Yorks.), Castle Rising (Norfolk), and Trim (Co. Meath, Ireland), with four great turrets, and wing-like projections in the middle of each side (Pl. 33).

The large rectangular keeps just described are, however, only a part of the whole group of rectangular stone keeps, most of which are of more modest dimensions. They vary from 32 ft square (Clitheroe, Lancs., mentioned earlier), to about 75 ft square, with the average somewhere around 50 ft square. Keeps of

28   Rochester Castle, Kent.

this size have only a quarter of the ground area of larger keeps, *c.* 100 ft square, and the amount of accommodation they provided was correspondingly limited. A few of them stand on mottes and may be stone replacements of earlier timber keeps. On the other hand, the keep may have been built in stone from the beginning and deliberately sited on a motte. Any structural problems may have been overcome by extending the foundations downwards to natural ground level, so that the motte surrounded rather than supported the stone structure. This certainly happened at Skenfrith (Gwent), where the keep is, in fact, circular, and may well have happened with some of the square keeps on mottes. These include: Lydford (Devon), where the keep basement is buried in the low motte which means that its foundations cannot be far off ground level anyway; Brough (Cumbria) where the motte consists of the remains of two earlier towers, one of them Roman; Clitheroe (Lancs.), where the

motte, shaped by scarping, is entirely natural; Farnham (Surrey) where the original stone structure (51 ft square) seems to have been built from ground level with the material of the motte (later encased in a shell wall) piled against it; and Lincoln, where there are two mottes, one with a shell-keep (below, p. 102) and one with a small rectangular keep (*c.* 45 × 36 ft) occupying most of the summit. At Guildford (Surrey) and Clun (Salop) rectangular stone keeps have been built into the sides of mottes, rather than sited on top (Pl. 34).

The majority of the surviving rectangular stone keeps, however, appear to have been built, like the great keeps, on level ground. There are substantial visible remains of several dozen of these and probably remains of many more still buried. Among the best preserved examples are the rectangular keeps at Richmond (Yorks.) (Pl. 35), Porchester (Hants) (Pl. 23) and Hedingham (Essex). The keep at Richmond was built over an

29 The keep at Bamburgh, Northumberland.

original gateway, which was then blocked, the entrance being at first floor (second storey) level from the rampart walk of the surrounding curtain wall. The keep is *c*. 52 × 45 ft and still stands to its full height, to the top of the battlements of the corner towers. The keep at Porchester is somewhat larger (*c*. 58 × 56 ft) with an elaborate forebuilding to the east. It too is preserved, in part, to the top of the

battlements on one side. The whole castle, keep and bailey, was built in one corner of the earlier Roman Saxon Shore fort (above, p. 68). Hedingham (Essex) is of similar dimensions to Porchester and still stands four storeys high, with two corner turrets rising another 20 ft. It had a forebuilding giving access at second storey level, with the great hall occupying the third storey where there was a mural

30 The keep at Norham, Northumberland.

gallery with its own row of windows. There was a fourth storey above the gallery, served by the topmost row of windows. Among the remaining square stone keeps worthy of mention are Appleby, Carlisle and Brougham (Cumbria) (Pl. 36), Carrickfergus (Antrim, N. Ireland) (Pl. 37), Goodrich (Hereford. & Worcs.), Ludlow (Salop) (Pl. 38), Peveril (Derby.), Scarborough (Yorks.), and Dolwyddelan (Gwynedd) (Pl. 39).

Rectangular stone keeps, both large and small, were built in the late eleventh and the twelfth centuries. After about a century, however, new, non-rectangular types of keep began to be built, probably under the influence of European and Near Eastern ideas on fortification which reached Britain as a result of, among other

31 Corfe Castle, Dorset.

things, the Crusades. Although convenient internally for the disposition of rooms, the rectangular keep has certain disadvantages externally. The corners are vulnerable to undermining by an attacker because they can be tackled from two sides. Moreover, because of the angles again, it is difficult for a sentry on top of the keep to see exactly what is happening around the corners. These disadvantages can be largely, if not entirely, overcome by building polygonal and circular keeps, and such keeps were built in the later decades of the twelfth century, from c. 1160 onwards.

Polygonal keeps are rather less common

32   Kenilworth Castle, Warwickshire: the keep.

33   Trim Castle, Co. Meath.

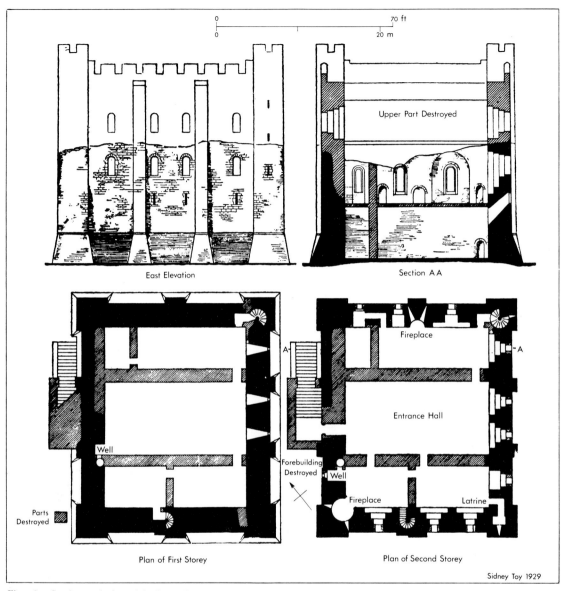

0   70 ft

0   20 m

East Elevation

Section A A

Upper Part Destroyed

Fireplace

Entrance Hall

Well

Forebuilding
Destroyed

Well

Fireplace

Latrine

Parts
Destroyed

Plan of First Storey

Plan of Second Storey

Sidney Toy 1929

Fig. 18. Section and plan of the keep, Canterbury Castle, Kent.

than circular keeps, and both are very much in a minority as compared with rectangular keeps. The keep at Odiham (Hants) is octagonal in plan with a buttress at each of the eight angles. The walls, *c.* 9 ft thick, enclose a space *c.* 40 ft across and the three storeys rose to a height of some 50 ft, with entry at second storey level. There is a smaller octagonal keep at Chilham (Kent), and the base of a much larger ten-sided keep, *c.* 70 ft wide, at Athlone (Westmeath, Ireland). The best preserved and most unusual of the polygonal keeps is Orford (Suffolk). It has so many sides (theoretically about twenty), that it is very nearly circular in plan, and the interior space is, in fact, circular. The exterior is dominated by three rectangular turrets, which rise well above the top of the keep and, together with a forebuilding between two of them, mask much of the outer face of the tower.

Purely circular keeps were rather more common than the polygonal type. One of the outstanding examples is the circular keep which forms the central feature of Pembroke Castle (Dyfed). It stands on a massive plinth and its walls, *c.* 15 ft thick, rise to a height of 80 ft; it has an overall diameter of 53 ft. It is of four storeys, the uppermost roofed with a stone dome 30 ft high at the centre. Externally there were

34   Clun Castle, Shropshire: the keep.

two fighting terraces, the uppermost around the top of the dome. Below and outside this was a second terrace or rampart walk on top of the main walls.

Like Orford (above) the exterior of Conisbrough (South Yorks.) is heavily obscured, in this case by six massive buttresses which rise to the full height of the tower. The buttresses, each *c.* 15 ft wide and 8 ft deep, occupy more than half the total external surface (Fig. 19). The keep is of four storeys with entrance at second storey level above a stone-domed basement. The walls are 15 ft thick, increasing to 20 ft at the base of the plinth. As at Pembroke there are two rampart walks, in this case one immediately above the other. Unlike most keeps which use spiral staircases for vertical communication, Conisbrough had a mural staircase rising concentrically in the thickness of the wall, rather like the staircase of a broch tower (above, p. 40). There are other well-preserved remains of circular keeps at Barnard Castle (Durham), Dolbadarn (Gwynedd) (Pl. 40),

35   The keep at Richmond Castle, Yorkshire.

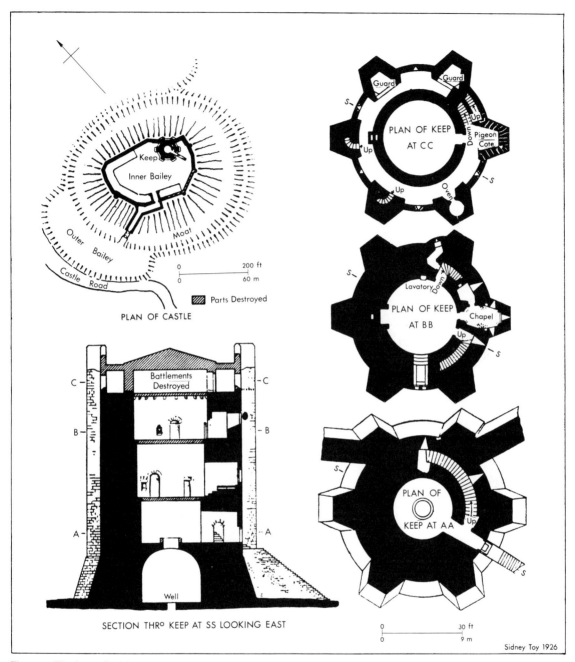

Fig. 19.   The keep, Conisbrough Castle, South Yorkshire.

Dundrum (Co. Down, Ireland), Longtown (Hereford. & Worcs.), Nenagh (Tipperary, Ireland) (Pl. 41), and Caldicot and Skenfrith (Gwent). There is, in addition, at least one D-shaped keep at Ewloe (Clwyd), which falls somewhere between the rectangular and circular types (Pl. 43).

36　Brougham Castle, Cumbria.

37　Carrickfergus Castle, Co. Antrim.

38   Ludlow Castle, Shropshire: the keep from the courtyard.

39   Dolwyddelan Castle, Gwynedd.

The keeps at Pontefract (Yorks.) and Clifford's Tower (York city) are unusual in being built on a quatrefoil plan. At Pontefract only the base of the keep remains but it appears to have consisted of a basically circular tower 77 ft in diameter with 12 ft thick walls, with four very large lobes, each *c.* 40 ft wide and 20 ft deep placed on the four cardinal points. As at Conisbrough access to the upper floors was by means of a mural staircase. Nothing is known of the upper storeys although a tower over 100 ft wide at the base must have risen to something like the same in overall height, providing space for the usual three or four storeys. Clifford's Tower in York is entirely quatrefoil in plan, both internally and externally, and it is very well preserved. It stands on top of a large motte, *c.* 100 ft in diameter at the top and is 80 ft wide overall with walls

40   The round keep at Dolbadarn, Gwynedd.

41   Nenagh Castle, Tipperary: the round keep.

42 Bothwell Castle, Strathclyde.

43 The D-shaped keep at Ewloe, Clwyd.

44   Clifford's Tower, York.

9 ft thick (Pl. 44). As a keep it was relatively low, only *c.* 40 ft high, with room for only two storeys. Entry was at ground floor level through a forebuilding which was virtually only a porch. The whole interior is now open to the sky but originally the first floor and the roof above were supported by a central pier. It is likely that the floors were subdivided into a number of separate rooms, probably four in each case, corresponding with the four lobes of the quatrefoil plan.

Both Pontefract and Clifford's Tower are late in the history of keeps, dating to the thirteenth century. Before dealing with other thirteenth-century developments, which involve the abandonment of the keep as an element in fortification, there is one other Norman type to be dealt with, the shell-keep. A shell-keep consists of a circular, oval or polygonal wall with the living accommodation built against its inner face, leaving an open courtyard in the centre (Fig. 17). A shell-keep is an enclosure rather than a building, and as such, its height is usually relatively low, as compared with its diameter. Whereas

many rectangular and round keeps were higher than they were wide, the average shell-keep appears to be only a quarter to one-third of the diameter in height. Many shell-keeps stand on mottes and may be replacements in stone of original timber structures. They can be seen as stone versions of the timber palisade around the top of the mound, with the accommodation now provided along the inside of the wall rather than in a keep. However, not all shell-keeps are later replacements of earlier timber structures. Some at least appear to have been built within the first few decades of the conquest, and shell-keeps must be seen as part of the repertoire of Norman fortification techniques. Some of them were built on level ground and are, in fact, stone equivalents of the ringworks mentioned in an earlier section (above, p. 80).

An excellent example of a shell-keep built on level ground is provided by Restormel Castle (Cornwall). The castle was built *c.* 1100, although at that time, it is suggested, it was an earth and timber structure. However, the traditional building material in Cornwall has always been stone, even in prehistoric times, and there is no reason why Restormel could not have been stone-built from the outset. If it was not built in stone then, it was certainly rebuilt in stone during the twelfth century. The rectangular bailey and the extensive buildings it contained are now gone but the shell-keep and its surrounding ditch are very well preserved. The shell-keep is formed by a wall 25 ft high above internal ground level and 8 ft thick, surrounding a circular space 109 ft in diameter, with an overall diameter of

126 ft. Although it is quite clear from the inside that the shell wall stands on level ground, externally the castle looks as if it is standing on a low motte. This is the result of piling the material from the ditch against the shell wall so that it looks as if the keep is standing on top of the earthwork rather than behind it. However, there is no doubt that Restormel was built on level, natural ground.

Apart from the main shell wall the structure consists of a porch-like entrance, a single rectangular tower on the opposite side, and a two-storey range of buildings, concentric with the walls, leaving a central courtyard about 65 ft in diameter. Access to the upper floor and to the rampart

Fig. 20   Half-plan and section of a shell-keep.

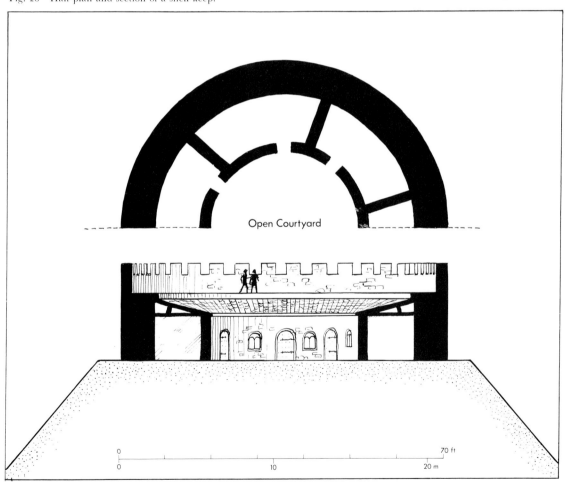

Open Courtyard

0   10   20 m
0   70 ft

45   The shell-keep at Rothesay, Bute.

walk and battlements, which are well preserved, is by means of two staircases situated on either side of the entrance.

Rothesay (Bute, Scotland) is an even larger shell-keep, slightly oval in plan (*c.* 180 × 150 ft overall), with walls 9 ft thick and over 20 ft high as originally built (Pl. 45). It has a more elaborate entrance than Restormel and four (later) circular towers around the shell wall. Internally its buildings are more haphazardly arranged than Restormel although the same broad principle of a central courtyard is observed.

Apart from Restormel and Rothesay, the majority of shell-keeps stand on mottes, whether natural or man-made, often of considerable size. In fact, it is true to say that where there are still stone remains on top of a motte they are frequently of the shell-keep type. An outstanding example of a shell-keep on a motte (probably a natural hillock shaped by scarping) is provided by the Round Tower, the central feature of Windsor Castle (Berks.). The upper half of the tower is a nineteenth-century addition but the lower half is a shell-keep of Henry II, *c.* 1175, roughly circular in plan, *c.* 100 ft in overall diameter. This contained a range of internal timber buildings although their exact plan is not known. They were replaced *c.* 1350 by a two-storey timber range against the internal wall, with a central rectangular courtyard, and this range still forms the basis of the present day interior arrangement. However, there appear to be the remains of a still earlier shell-keep around the base of Henry II's structure, dating probably to the early days of the conquest. This was about 128 ft in overall diameter with walls about 12 ft thick. Henry II built his shell-keep immediately inside this so that the earlier shell-keep now forms the terrace which can be seen surrounding the base of the Round Tower. The latter was only the central feature of what eventually became a large and complex castle with two very large baileys, one to the east of the motte and one to the west (above).

Equally striking and well preserved is the shell-keep which forms the nucleus of Durham Castle, the residence of the Bishop of Durham, alongside the great Norman cathedral. The octagonal shell-keep (largely if not entirely rebuilt in the nineteenth century) measures $c.\ 80 \times 65$ ft

46 Tamworth Castle, Staffordshire: the shell-keep.

47 Berkeley Castle, Gloucestershire.

and stands on a motte (*c.* 250 ft in diameter at the base) which is probably largely, if not entirely, natural. To the west is a large triangular bailey containing extensive buildings of the twelfth and thirteenth centuries.

The polygonal (twelve-sided) shell-keep at Cardiff stands on a motte (*c.* 220 ft in diameter at the base), built in one corner of a late Roman fort, one of the so called Saxon Shore forts (above, pp. 66–9). The twelve-sided shell-keep is about 90 ft in overall diameter. Other shell-keeps, mostly on mottes, include Arundel (Sussex, with considerable baileys to north and south, as at Windsor); Berkhamsted (Herts.); Carisbrooke (Isle of Wight); Lewes (Sussex) with, in fact, two shell-keeps on two separate mottes; Launceston (Cornwall), with a thirteenth-century round tower built inside the shell wall; Tamworth (Staffs.), still substantially intact to the battlements (Pl. 46); Totnes (Devon); Tonbridge (Kent); Warwick Castle (War.), where the shell-keep and motte now form part of a larger and later castle; and Berkeley Castle (Glos.) (Pl. 47).

4 Later Medieval Castles and Town Walls

In broad terms the developments just outlined (timber motte-and-bailey castles, square, round and polygonal stone keeps and shell-keeps) took place in the two centuries or so following the conquest of 1066. Subsequently, as already indicated, many of the then existing castles were added to, to meet the demand for more space and greater comfort, and in response to new ideas on fortification. However, new ideas on fortification also found expression in entirely new castles in which the idea of the keep, of whatever form, was largely abandoned in favour of a different principle of defence, involving greater emphasis on one or more curtain walls, on more regular layout, on wall towers, and on gatehouses which, in a sense, were a replacement of the keep. These developments were all outstandingly exemplified during the reign of Edward I (1272–1307), one of the most brilliant castle-building periods in British history, but already earlier in the century, even while castles with keeps were still being built, there was clear evidence of new thinking, both in newly built castles and in additions to existing castles.

Castles

Beeston Castle (Ches.), built *c.* 1225, has no keep. Spectacularly situated on the end of a high promontory overlooking the Cheshire plain, it consists of inner and outer baileys, each protected by a curtain wall with towers at regular intervals, and twin-towered gatehouses at the two entrances, although the outer entrance is largely destroyed. The inner gatehouse consists of two D-shaped towers with the gateway between, linked at the first floor level to provide accommodation equivalent to that of a keep; no doubt there were other buildings in the inner bailey, as well as three other wall towers. The towers on the outer curtain wall, more than half of which is destroyed, are semi-circular and open at the back.

Beeston was somewhat irregular in plan, due probably to the irregularities of the site. In other sites of this period, however, the desire for a more regular layout is quite evident, as is the preference for circular towers projecting well beyond the curtain, particularly at the corners, to provide flanking fire along the adjacent walls. Bothwell Castle (Strathclyde), built *c.* 1242, still has a circular keep (Pl. 42), but the curtain wall of the bailey is laid out in straight lines and the circular corner towers project for about two-thirds of their circumference beyond the wall. There is also a twin-towered gatehouse. The same features appear even more clearly in two other castles, Barnwell (Northants.) and Inverlochy (Highland county). Barnwell is basically very simple in plan, a rectangle (*c.* 180 × 120 ft overall) formed by a curtain wall 12 ft thick and 30 ft high. The four corner towers (three round and one **D**-shaped) project boldly, and there is a gatehouse formed by two **D**-shaped towers which project 20 ft beyond the line of the curtain wall. The ditch which originally surrounded the site has now gone. Inverlochy Castle is equally simple. The early portion (there is a fifteenth-century outer wall) consists of a rectangular curtain wall *c.* 9 ft thick enclosing a space *c.* 100 × 90 ft with a large circular tower (*c.* 30 ft diameter) at each corner, projecting for three-quarters of its circumference. There were two entrances but neither formed part of a gatehouse, and the whole site was originally surrounded by a ditch.

Generally similar features appear at one or two other sites as well. The outer bailey at Pembroke Castle (above, p. 95), added between 1200 and 1250, has the same boldly projecting circular towers along its curtain wall and a gatehouse between twin towers. Skenfrith which, like Pembroke, had a circular stone keep as its nucleus, was either built with, or had added to it, a bailey very much on the lines of Barnwell and Inverlochy: a four-sided (trapeze-shaped) curtain wall, *c.* 8 ft thick, four boldly projecting circular corner towers, and a gatehouse, now destroyed, all surrounded by a wet moat fed from the River Monnow. At Helmsley Castle (Yorks.) the **D**-shaped keep is attached to the curtain wall of the bailey which is trapeze-shaped in plan (*c.* 320 × 220 ft), with projecting circular corner towers and an entrance between two **D**-shaped towers. Criccieth Castle (Gwynedd) also belongs originally to this period (*c.* 1250). Although it lacks projecting towers it has, in addition to its plain curtain wall, a massive, twin-towered gatehouse. It was, shortly afterwards, adapted by Edward I to form part of his system of fortifications for North Wales, during an intensive period of castle building which crystallized the various developments just outlined, and

marked the culmination of castle building in the British Isles and in Europe.

Edward I came to the throne in 1272 with great experience, both at home and abroad, of warfare, siege and fortification. A dozen or more important castles built during his reign (1272–1307) bear witness to his experience and to the new ideas on fortification which had been developing during the thirteenth century. As indicated earlier in discussing timber motte-and-bailey castles (pp. 81–4), Wales was a permanent trouble spot for the English kings and much of Edward's castle-building effort was directed towards the pacification and control of the country, most particularly North Wales. An integral part of his policy was the establishment of colonies of loyal citizens among his recalcitrant Welsh subjects, and to this end many of the new castles were accompanied by walled towns, two of which, Conway and Caernarvon, are among the best preserved walled towns in Europe (below, pp. 133–5).

Edward's conquest of North Wales began effectively in 1277, and in the same year he set in train the building of Flint Castle (Pl. 48). During the next ten years he built further castles, at Rhuddlan, Conway, Caernarvon, Harlech, Beaumaris, and re-utilized the existing castle at Criccieth. The eventual result was a ring of castles around North Wales which hemmed it in on three sides, and which could all be supplied and reinforced by sea and were not, therefore, dependent on land communication through potentially hostile territory.

The first of Edward's castles in North Wales was Flint, and it was also the most unusual. Although it reflected the changing pattern of thirteenth-century fortification (regular, rectangular plan, boldly projecting corner towers) it also has, somewhat strangely for its date of 1277, a keep of circular plan (Fig. 18, d). The keep is separated from the inner bailey by its own moat, and is of unusual design with a double shell wall, *c.* 71 ft in

48 Flint Castle, Clwyd.

overall diameter. The keep takes the place of the south-east corner tower. The inner bailey is roughly rectangular (c. 190 × 170 ft overall), with walls c. 10 ft thick and circular projecting towers (40 ft in diameter) at the three remaining corners (Pl. 48). There is also an outer bailey on the landward side, and there was originally an earth-and-timber town wall, linked to the castle, of which all trace has now gone.

In the same year (1277) Edward moved forward from Flint to Rhuddlan on the River Clwyd, where he quickly brought about the surrender of the Welsh leader Llywelyn ap Gruffydd. There was already a timber motte-and-bailey castle there (the mound of which is still visible, to the south-east of the stone castle), and no doubt this was used while the new castle was being built. The master mason-cum-military engineer responsible, under Edward, for the building of Rhuddlan, as indeed for Flint and the other Edwardian castles in North Wales, was James of St George, who had worked on the building of many castles in France and Switzerland, including St Georges-d'Espéranche, from which he took his name. The castle was designed on what is now called the concentric plan and consisted basically of an inner curtain wall, surrounded by an outer curtain wall, surrounded by a ditch, surrounded finally by a timber palisade, forming successive lines of defence (Fig. 18, c); more elaborate versions of this concentric arrangement will be encountered at Harlech and Beaumaris (below pp. 114–17). The inner ward or bailey (c. 150 × 130 ft internally) is diamond shaped in plan and is surrounded by a curtain wall, c. 9 ft thick, with six circular towers some 40 ft in diameter, four of which form two twin-towered gatehouses at opposite corners of the enclosure. Towers and walls are preserved very nearly to their original heights. The curtain wall of the outer bailey, which must have been much lower anyway, has mostly gone, except for its lower section where it forms the inner

facing of the ditch. The outer side of the ditch was also faced with stone and above it, forming the outermost obstacle, was a timber palisade. The ditch was nearly 50 ft wide and c. 15 ft deep and enclosed the castle on three sides. On the fourth, south-western side there is a steep natural slope to the river, enclosed by a triangular extension of the outer curtain wall which runs down to a dock gate with a projecting rectangular tower, Gillot's Tower. To the north-west of the new castle was a new town, defended by an earth-and-timber rampart (the north-west portion of which survives), to which English settlers were attracted by low rentals. The present High Street and the streets at right angles to it indicate the street plan of the original town.

By the beginning of 1283 Edward had completed the conquest of Snowdonia and had moved from Rhuddlan, which must by then have been nearing completion, to Conway, where almost immediately plans were put in hand for a new castle. Again James of St George was in overall charge of the building work. Because of the nature of the site—a great knoll of rock—there was no question of any concentric arrangement here (Fig. 18, b). The basic plan was very simple: eight great drum towers linked by a curtain wall, with barbicans covering the eastern and western entrances, but the result was one of the most formidable and impressive castles in medieval Europe. The four eastern towers (c. 40 ft in diameter), each surmounted by a turret (Pl. 49), define the inner ward, cut off from the remainder of the castle by a cross wall, with a narrow entrance and (originally) a drawbridge. The inner ward (c. 80 × 70 ft) contained the royal apartments. Apart from the entrance from the outer ward, there was a separate entrance, covered by an outwork or barbican, on the east, giving access via the watergate from beyond the town wall. The main entrance of the outer ward, on the other hand, opened from within the town wall, although it too was covered by

49 Towers and turrets at Conway Castle, Gwynedd.

a barbican, approached by a long ramp with a drawbridge at its head. The outer ward is much larger than the inner and contained the great hall and the other buildings necessary for normal occupation—kitchens, stables, cellars, guard rooms and so on. Curtain wall, towers and turrets are preserved virtually to their original height. As completed they were limewashed so that the whiteness of the whole structure must have made a striking contrast with the dark green of the hills in the background. Conway Castle stands in one corner of the walled town of Conway which was built simultaneously with it as part of Edward's policy of establishing pockets of loyal English settlers among the Welsh (below, p. 115).

Caernarvon, begun at the same time as Conway (1283) is very much the same sort

of castle, a high curtain wall linking a series of massive polygonal towers and two twin-towered gatehouses, subdivided into inner and outer wards, not so much by a wall as by a whole building, although this was apparently not completed. As at Conway there are no outer concentric defences, nor indeed are there any barbicans covering the entrances (Fig. 21, a). Again, as at Conway, the curtain wall, the towers and the gatehouses are virtually intact and stand to their original height. The curtain wall is some 15 ft thick and 55 ft high, and on the river side (to the south) contains two mural passages, one above the other, both with arrow slits, which together with the rampart walk at the top, would have provided space for three tiers of defenders in case of attack. The most massive of the towers is the

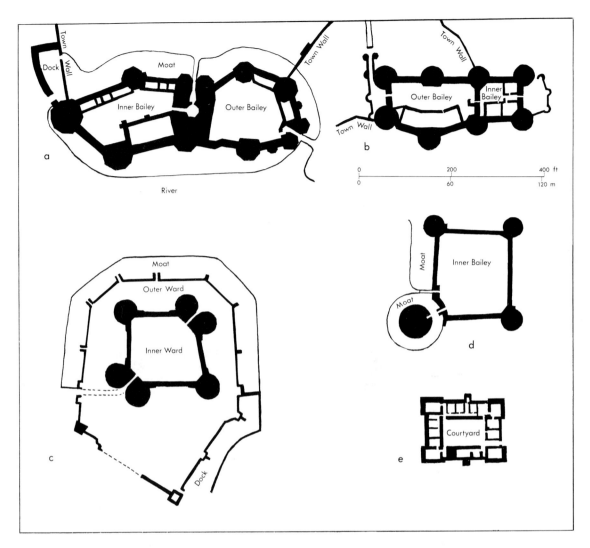

Fig. 21 Outline plans of castles: (a) Caernarvon;
(b) Conway; (c) Rhuddlan; (d) Flint; (e) Bolton.

Eagle Tower (*c.* 75 ft in diameter) which is
effectively a self-contained keep, providing a
final refuge even if the inner ward were
over-run (Pl. 50). It has three turrets and
a means of escape (a water gate), at a
point beyond the town walls and adjacent
to the entrance to a small dock. The
King's Gate, on the town side, had an
arrangement not dissimilar to Denbigh
Castle (below), in which the entrance
passage between twin towers runs into a
chamber from which the only exit is
another passage, at right angles, leading to
the interior, in this case to the inner
bailey. This elaborate gatehouse which
should have divided the inner from the
outer ward does not appear to have been
completed. The outer ward was entered
from outside the town wall via the
Queen's Gate.

Like Conway, Caernarvon was the work
of James of St George. In the next castle
to be considered, however, James and his

50 The Eagle Tower, Caernarvon Castle, Gwynedd.

51　The gatehouse, Harlech Castle, Gwynedd.

master, Edward I, adopted again the concentric layout seen already at Rhuddlan. Harlech (begun in 1283) is a classic example of the type. The (nearly) rectangular inner bailey (c. 165 × 130 ft) is defined by a curtain wall 9–12 ft thick, four circular projecting corner towers, and a powerful gatehouse which, like the Eagle Tower at Caernarvon, acted as a keep and final refuge, capable of surviving independently of the rest of the castle. The middle bailey was more in the nature of a terrace, its curtain wall following closely, within 10–30 ft, the line of the inner curtain wall. Beyond the outer curtain on the south and east was a wide moat. On the north and west the ground fell away steeply and much of it was included in an irregular outer bailey on the west side of which, well below the main castle, was a water gate. Although not quite so well preserved as Conway and Caernarvon, Harlech is substantially intact, particularly as regards the inner curtain wall, the corner towers and the impressive gatehouse (Pl. 51).

The last of Edward's castles in North Wales, Beaumaris, in Anglesey, was also on the concentric plan, and probably the most elaborate example of all (Pls. 52, 53). It was begun in 1295 as an addition to the system, after Caernarvon had been (temporarily) captured by the Welsh during the uprising of 1294. The plan of the inner bailey is symmetrical because there are no physical limitations on the site, and the outer bailey nearly so. The inner bailey (c. 195 × 180 ft) has four projecting corner towers, two D-shaped intermediate towers in the east and west walls and two great gatehouses similar to the one at Harlech, on the north and south walls. The polygonal curtain wall of the outer bailey has four circular corner towers, eight circular intermediate towers and north and south gateways, in each case offset from the north and south inner entrances. There is a dock next to the south entrance. The associated walled town lay to the west with the south entrance within the circuit and the north

entrance outside it. In spite of the elaborate plan, however, Beaumaris Castle was never finished. Although the plan is more or less complete the upper portions of the gatehouses and towers were left unfinished, occasioning a good deal of repair work in later years, of which there are numerous reports.

Denbigh Castle was not an integral part of Edward's system for North Wales, but it belongs to the period and displays the same ideas on fortification. It was built by Henry de Lacy, Earl of Lincoln, to whom the area was granted by Edward I. He cut off the south-west corner of the town wall, begun in 1282, which thus forms the southern and western side of the castle. The northern and eastern sides were formed by an arc of curtain wall with three octagonal towers and a massive gatehouse, formed of three further octagonal towers in a triangular arrangement. The octagonal towers recall Caernarvon as does the layout of the gatehouse.

Castle building in the second half of the thirteenth century was not, however, confined to North Wales. Many other castles were built in these decades exemplifying the defence principles just outlined, most notably that of the concentric plan. Caerphilly Castle (Mid Glam.) is an elaborate structure, the central portion of which is a concentric arrangement, similar to Harlech and Beaumaris, standing originally on an island in a lake held in on one side by a dam which was also a great barbican, nearly 1000 ft long, protecting the approach from the east (Pl. 54). There are gateways on to the dam at either end and at the centre, via a drawbridge, and access to the castle proper, on the island, by means of another drawbridge. The inner bailey is of the usual rectangular form, c. 200 × 150 ft with boldly projecting corner towers and two twin-towered gatehouses in the east and west walls. The curtain wall of the outer bailey, which follows closely the plan of the inner, is plain, without

52　The outer entrance, Beaumaris Castle, Anglesey.

53   The moat and outer curtain wall, Beaumaris Castle.

54 Caerphilly Castle, Mid Glamorgan: the barbican.

towers, except for those of the two gatehouses, on the eastern and western side, opposite the inner gatehouses. In front of the western entrance is another outwork, in the form of an island with a curtain wall, covering the western approach just as the dam-barbican covered the eastern. All in all Caerphilly, with its concentric inner castle, its two great outworks and its water defences, is a most formidable structure, far removed in concept from even the most elaborate motte-and-bailey castles of earlier periods.

Kidwelly Castle (Dyfed) and Goodrich Castle (Hereford. & Worcs.), both built *c.* 1280–1310, embody the concentric principle in simpler form, due to the limitations of the sites. At Kidwelly the outer curtain wall is **D**-shaped in plan, the straight eastern side standing on a high river bank (Pl. 55). The main gatehouse is at the southern angle with a lesser gatehouse at the north. The rectangular inner bailey has its eastern wall in common with the outer curtain wall so that it was surrounded on only three sides by the outer bailey, on the north, west and south. At Goodrich there are steep falls to the river on two sides, north and west, but it is on these sides that the outer bailey exists (Fig. 22). On the south and east the wide, rock-cut moat lies directly beneath

the inner bailey wall. The latter embraces an earlier rectangular keep and has its gatehouse at the north-east corner, replacing the normal, projecting corner tower. In front of the gatehouse, across the moat, is a **D**-shaped barbican, reached from the outside by a drawbridge across a curving extension of the moat. Other castles of the period include Aberystwyth (Dyfed) built on the concentric plan, of which little now remains, and Caerlaverock (Dumfries & Galloway) (Pl. 56), unusual because of its triangular plan with a twin-towered gatehouse at one of

Fig. 22   Plan of Goodrich Castle, Hereford & Worcs.

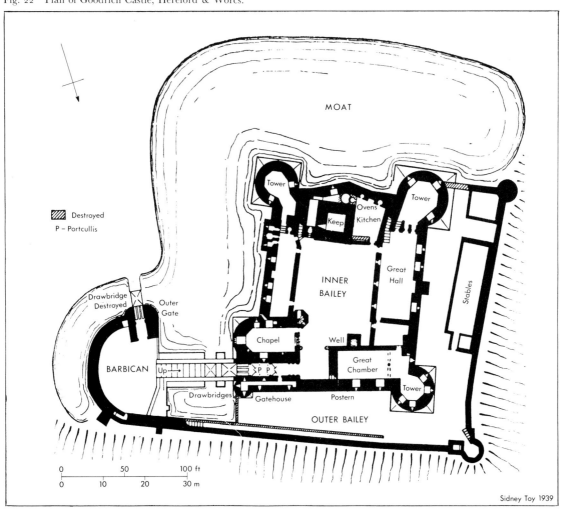

55   Kidwelly Castle, Dyfed.

the angles. There is no outer bailey, the triangular enclosure being surrounded by two moats with an earth bank between.

Edward I was also largely responsible for the work which brought the Tower of London to its present shape. The original keep, the White Tower, was surrounded by a curtain wall forming a middle bailey *c.* 1190. Edward rebuilt this wall and added another curtain wall just beyond, forming an outer bailey and making the arrangement effectively concentric (Fig. 23). At the south-west angle he provided an elaborate entrance with a **D**-shaped barbican, very much on the lines of the entrance at Goodrich Castle, mentioned above.

The Edwardian period was the climax of medieval castle building with predominantly military considerations in mind. Although many castles were built during the fourteenth and even fifteenth centuries there was an increasing interest in, and emphasis on, the more domestic aspects of the accommodation provided. Castles had always been domestic to some

degree, but domestic considerations came a poor second to those of defence during the eleventh to thirteenth centuries. In the fourteenth and subsequent centuries, however, the demand for more space and greater comfort is quite evident in the plan of new castles and the additions to existing ones. In the new structures the appearance is still very much that of a stronghold, but internally they are houses, and the term fortified houses instead of castles becomes increasingly appropriate as time goes on.

Fortified Houses

The plans of such 'domestic castles' or 'fortified houses' are to be found in the inner baileys of concentric castles such as Harlech, Beaumaris, Caerphilly and Goodrich. Bodiam Castle (Sussex), built nearly a century later, follows the same general lines but is, in fact, a very different concept (Pl. 60). It has the rectangular plan, the boldly projecting circular corner towers, rectangular

56 Caerlaverock Castle, Dumfries & Galloway.

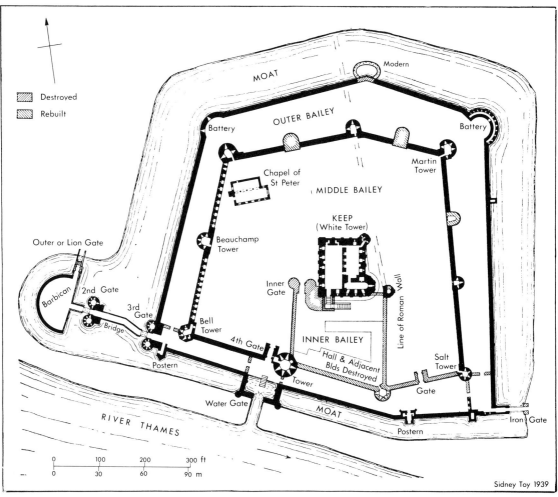

Fig. 23   Plan of the Tower of London.

intermediate towers and a gatehouse. It has a barbican covering the entrance and stands in a wide rectangular moat. Thus far it is, and looks, thoroughly military. Internally, however, it is a very different story. Within the curtain wall what exists is, in fact, a rectangular courtyard house, with the plan and features to be encountered in later courtyard houses with few, if any, military pretensions. The buildings ranged around the courtyard are two storeys in height. The south range, opposite the gatehouse, contains the great hall, the screens passage, the buttery and the pantry, with a passage between the

two latter leading to the kitchen. The east range contained the private family accommodation and the chapel, the west range the domestic offices and servants' quarters. This is a standard domestic arrangement to be found in dozens of medieval and early post-medieval houses. The north range contained the gatehouse, and the military quarters, but this was no military establishment such as Harlech, Caernarvon or Conway. The emphasis had changed, even if the external architecture gave little indication of it. This is a domestic establishment, a family house, but one in which there was still a need to preserve both a martial exterior and some accommodation for the military.

In Bolton Castle (Yorks.), also built in the latter part of the fourteenth century, there is even more emphasis on the domestic aspect. The plan is much more compact, now with rectangular corner towers, projecting only slightly, and no gatehouse (Fig. 18, e). It is much further away from the Edwardian plan than Bodiam. The rectangular corner towers are five storeys high, the rest of the buildings three storeys. The main accommodation is at first floor level where the great hall, the kitchen, the chapel and the private family quarters occupy much of the north, west and south ranges. The east range, incorporating the entrance passage, was given over largely to the defence force. In spite of its impressive height Bolton Castle is far less military looking externally than Bodiam, and certainly a long way removed from any of the great Edwardian castles. Its relatively plain

external walls are simply a secure cladding for a large domestic establishment. Other Yorkshire castles of the same period, at Wressle and Sherriff Hutton, tell the same story. Both were built on the rectangular plan with domestic considerations very much to the fore, although they are not nearly so well preserved as Bolton Castle.

The pattern of the late fourteenth century is continued into the fifteenth century with perhaps the most celebrated example, Herstmonceux in Sussex, built in 1441. Herstmonceux is a large rectangular building (c. 219 × 208 ft), brick-built and surrounded by a moat. It has a formidable array of octagonal towers and crenellated walls, and an impressive gatehouse to the exterior. Internally, however, the arrangements were thoroughly domestic. Although the interior was completely rebuilt in recent times, the original plans exist and show that there were two storey ranges on all four sides defining a courtyard. The great hall, however,

57 Chepstow Castle, Gwent.

58   Carisbrooke Castle, Isle of Wight: the gatehouse.

59 The gatehouse, Skipton Castle, Yorkshire.

60 Bodiam Castle, Sussex.

formed a range across the middle of the courtyard, and a similar arrangement is found in other castles (below) and in some houses, Haddon Hall (Derby.) for example. The main advantage of this position is that the hall can have large windows in both long walls, which would not be possible against the curtain wall. Compton Castle (Devon) (1420) and Kirby Muxloe (Leics.) (1480) follow the same general plan. Compton is surrounded by a high curtain wall but the internal buildings which form two courtyards do not abut directly against it except on the north side. The great hall, now destroyed, again occupied the range between the two courtyards. At Kirby Muxloe the castle of 1480 was built around an earlier manor house, but in such a way as to leave the great hall across the middle of the courtyard thus formed, in the same arrangement as Compton and Herstmonceux. Like the latter, Kirby Muxloe was brick-built, although in a much simpler style, with square towers at each corner and a gatehouse in the north front.

The castles just described were largely or entirely new foundations of the fourteenth and fifteenth centuries, and as such reflected fully the current attitudes with regard to domestic comfort in fortified premises. Such new castles were, however, greatly outnumbered by existing castles where, for simple economic reasons, it was not possible to build entirely afresh. In such cases the demand for greater domestic space and comfort was met by additions to the existing fabric, and this practice goes a long way to explaining the great variety in the appearance of British castles as we see them now. Most frequently the additions took the form of new towers which, with their many floor levels, added greatly to the amount of accommodation available. An excellent example of this is provided by the late fourteenth-century developments at Warwick Castle.

The original castle consisted of a shell-keep with a large bailey on its north-eastern side. In the later decades of the fourteenth century a new section of curtain wall was built at the north-eastern end with a tall tower at each angle and a powerful gatehouse in the middle. The two towers, Caesar's Tower and Guy's Tower (Pl. 61), were formidable pieces of work which provided both security and a considerable amount of accommodation. Caesar's Tower, over 130 ft high above external ground level, has, in addition to a basement prison and guardroom accommodation at the top, no less than three suites of rooms, each on a separate floor, consisting of a main room ($c.$ 20 × 15 ft) with a fireplace and windows, a smaller, mural chamber (bedroom?) on one side and a latrine on the other (Fig. 24). Guy's Tower (128 ft high) with fewer floors overall, neverthless has no less than four suites of rooms of the same general type. These tower rooms would probably form a series of private apartments. At the same time a large range of more general accommodation was added to the north-east side of the bailey, including a great hall, kitchen, servants' quarters, chapel and so on. Further additions were made in the fifteenth century (a tower with four turrets on the north side), and in the sixteenth (a water gate on the south side of the bailey). There is a similar arrangement of four superimposed suites of rooms in a rectangular tower ($c.$ 40 × 30 ft) at Ludlow, projecting beyond the curtain wall of the inner bailey on the north side, built $c.$ 1330. A tower as impressive externally as Caesar's Tower stands at the north-west corner of Caister Castle (Norfolk). It rises to nearly 100 ft, well above the height of the remaining brick-built structure, and looks like an addition to the original rectangular castle enclosing a courtyard.

Tower-houses

Castles of the courtyard type, such as Bodiam, Bolton and Herstmonceux,

61 Guy's Tower, Warwick Castle.

described earlier, were not the only ones
built during the fourteenth and fifteenth
centuries. In the courtyard castles, as in
courtyard houses, the various rooms (great
hall, kitchen, private chambers, servants'
quarters) were disposed laterally, that is,
they were side by side on one or, at the
most, two floors. In another group of
castles, however, built or added to during
the same period the rooms are arranged
vertically, one above the other, forming a
tower four or five storeys high, and since
they embrace the full range of domestic
accommodation, the term tower-house is
appropriate. As will be seen in Chapter 5,
tower-houses form one of the major types
of Scottish fortification, but there are a
few in England, some of them of very
striking appearance. The English examples
are easily distinguishable from the Scottish
examples but they observe the same
principle, that of a manor house placed, as
it were, on end, with the kitchen, servants'

quarters, great hall and private apartments
placed one above the other forming a
vertical arrangement—a tower—rather
than the more conventional horizontal
arrangement surrounding a courtyard.

One of the earliest examples in England
is Dudley Castle (Hereford. & Worcs.)
built c. 1320, very much the same sort of
date as tower-houses began in Scotland.
Dudley was a rebuild of an earlier castle
and was placed on the pre-existing
mound. It was oblong in plan with four
round corner towers and was two storeys
in height, lower than most of the tower-
houses to be described below. The ground
floor almost certainly housed the kitchen
and servants' quarters, while above there
was a hall with private apartments at one
end and a screens passage and pantry and
buttery at the other, that is, a normal
manor house arrangement. Nunney in
Somerset (c. 1373) is of generally similar
plan to Dudley but was four storeys in

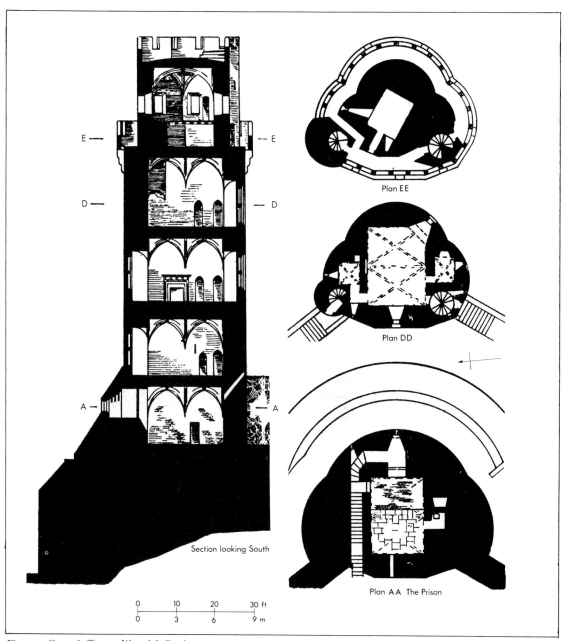

E — — E

D — — D

A — — A

Section looking South

Plan EE

Plan DD

Plan AA The Prison

| 0 | 10 | 20 | 30 ft |
| 0 | 3 | 6 | 9 m |

Fig. 24   Caesar's Tower, Warwick Castle.

height (Pl. 62). Each of the four floors was *c*. 60 × 25 ft and there were, in addition, four rooms (*c*. 12 ft diameter) at each level in each of the four corner towers. The two lower floors were probably given over to kitchens, storage and servants' quarters, while the great hall was on the third, with private apartments, chapel, etc. on the topmost floor. The tower was surrounded by a wide moat and stood within a large, roughly rectangular bailey (now destroyed), *c*. 400 ft square.

62   Nunney Castle, Somerset.

63 Warkworth Castle, Northumberland.

Warkworth (Northumb.) is one of the most unusual and elaborate of all tower-houses in England (Pl. 63). It is a rebuild (*c.* 1390) of an earlier keep, probably of the twelfth century. The new structure was basically square in plan (*c.* 80 × 80 ft), with a tower-like projection (*c.* 25 × 15 ft) at the centre of each face. Warkworth is equally unusual internally. Instead of the simple rectangular internal spaces of most tower-houses there is an intricate pattern of rooms, passages and staircases. The accommodation is on three main floors. The ground floor provides space for storage, a prison and a guardroom. On the first floor are the great hall, the kitchens and chapel, rising through two storeys, and the great chamber with a private parlour above, together with other private quarters and bedrooms, on the second floor. Externally the contrast with the great Norman keeps of earlier times is

demonstrated most strikingly by the ample provision of windows, particularly in the upper portions, and particularly for the great hall.

Raglan (Gwent) is more keep-like than anything considered so far, but its fifteenth-century date (1432–45) and its internal arrangements bring it into the tower-house group (Pl. 64). Like Nunney it is surrounded by its own moat, with the main part of the associated castle to one side. It is hexagonal in plan with a kitchen and service quarters in the lowest storey, a hall above, and private apartments and bedrooms above that.

Unquestionably the most striking tower-house in England is Tattershall Castle (Lincs.) (1433–48), surpassing even Warkworth. It is a brick-built rectangular structure (*c.* 80 × 60 ft overall), with four octagonal corner turrets which rise above the level of the main parapet, to a height of 120 ft. The building is of five storeys, including a basement. Above this the accommodation consists of four large rooms, one on each floor (*c.* 40 × 20 ft), with decorated fireplaces. The three upper rooms form a single suite and consist of a hall (first floor), audience chamber (second) and bed chamber (third). There is no kitchen, so presumably the tower was served from the original kitchens of the great hall in the inner ward. Although virtually everything apart from the tower-house has now gone, it is quite clear that its east face, at ground and first floor level, was masked by the original great hall which served the general needs of the castle. The three doors now visible in the east face of the tower at ground level were

64 Raglan Castle. Gwent.

65 Ashby-de-la-Zouch Castle, Leicestershire: the tower-house.

not, in fact, external doors. They were communicating doors between the existing buildings and the sumptuous brick-built addition of the fifteenth century. A not dissimilar tower on a smaller scale was built into the fortified palace of Buckden (Hunts.) by the Bishop of Lincoln, early in the second half of the century.

Towards the end of the century (c. 1474) another splendid tower-house, over 90 ft high, was built at Ashby-de-la-Zouch (Leics.). It was a four storey structure with basement, kitchen, great hall and great chamber, with additional accommodation in an attached wing (seven storeys), and in the corner turrets (Pl. 65).

Apart from the courtyard castles and tower-houses just described there was a considerable amount of building in the same period in the Anglo-Scottish border region, involving towers of various kinds, but these are best considered in the next chapter where northern towers and Scottish and Irish tower-houses form the main subject matter.

Town Walls

The question of medieval town walls has been touched on already in dealing with the Edwardian castles of North Wales. Conway and Caernarvon (Pls 66 and 67) have virtually intact circuits, but they are two of only a handful of sites with remains in such condition. For the most part town walls have been swept away, although there are a number of places where there is still a section of wall or an original gateway to be seen. However, the sum total of what survives, both complete circuits and otherwise, is only a fraction of the hundred or more towns in England and Wales which are known to have had enclosing walls.

The story of town defences fills some of the six-century gap between the Roman period and the introduction of castles by the Normans in 1066. Although, as pointed out in Chapter 2, the English had

no castles prior to this event, they were not without fortifications, in the form of walled towns, at least for some part of the period. Much of the evidence is written and relates only to the last two centuries or so before the Norman Conquest. However, it will be clear from what was said about the walls of Roman Chester (above, p. 69) that substantial portions remained standing throughout the Dark Age period, and this is likely to apply to other Roman sites as well. It seems very unlikely that the substantial range of stone-built Roman fortifications (in the case of the towns elaborately reorganized as late as AD 343), would not be made use of in time of danger. It is virtually certain, therefore, that for a couple of centuries after the Roman withdrawal, and longer in some cases, the surviving town and fortress walls, patched up and mended where necessary, met the needs of the native population for defence; this use of earlier works fills out the story of fortification in an otherwise poorly documented period. Apart from Chester itself, most if not all those present day towns which include -chester or -caster in their names must have gone through the same sort of process.

The documentary evidence referred to earlier indicates that during the last two centuries or so before the Norman Conquest there were over fifty towns in England and Wales which were fortified in one way or another. These must have included still surviving Roman works, no doubt by this time much altered and added to, but a large number of town walls would appear to have been entirely new undertakings, involving timber and earth defences rather than stone. In this they would have been very similar to Roman defences of the first century (i.e. before they were replaced with stone), consisting of a frontal ditch with the earth thrown inwards to form a rampart, either revetted with turf or timber or surmounted by a timber palisade. There is no evidence that towers or turrets were involved and gateways were probably of the simplest kind. Although many such systems were eventually given stone revetments, and other refinements such as towers and towered gateways, this was not universal. Some towns retained earthwork defences until quite late in the medieval period. At both Coventry (War.) and Sandwich (Kent) such defences were replaced by stone walls only in the fifteenth century. The two best surviving examples of pre-conquest earthwork town walls are Wallingford (Oxon.) and Wareham (Dorset), although the latter was, at a later stage, given a frontal stone wall to the rampart.

The town defences just considered were made necessary by the invasions of the ninth century AD and the consequent struggles between the English and the Danes. How far such defences were maintained once the immediate danger had passed is not known. It is unlikely, however, that all were maintained in a high state of readiness. The invasion of 1066 must have caused a further flurry of activity, although again, once that was over, there does not seem to have been much continuing concern about town defences. The Domesday survey of 1086 indicates that forty-eight towns were fortified (very much the same total as two centuries earlier), although what state the fortifications were in is not clear. Certainly by about the year 1200 the defences appear to have been beyond repair in more than half of these towns. It looks very much as if, in the century and a half after the conquest, town defences were not considered to be of any great importance, the emphasis being on castle building. After 1200, however, the situation changed, and it is from about this time that the story of stone-built town defences begins, including those which have survived to the present day.

There is some evidence of work on town defences in the later years of the twelfth century, under King Richard (1189–99), but the greatest stimulus seems to have been in the early decades of the thirteenth when the threat of invasion from both France and Wales led, as ever, to a renewed activity in the provision of town walls. In this case, however, the activity was not short-lived. During the remainder of the thirteenth century, and to a lesser degree during the following two centuries, there was a steady build-up in the number of town defences, and in their complexity, particularly with regard to towers and gateways. By 1500 there were very few towns of any importance which were not surrounded by defensive walls of some sort. Much of the documentary evidence comes from the record of what are known as 'murage grants'. This was the granting, by the king, of permission to levy a toll on goods coming into the town, the proceeds of which were to be used for the provision of a town wall, gates and so on. Murage grants are recorded for about half (51) of the 108 walled towns in the thirteenth century, starting in 1220, under Henry III (1216–72) and Edward I (1272–1307). In addition to these 51 there were also the walled towns of North Wales established by Edward I and financed directly by the crown rather than by a levy on goods. The most notable surviving examples of these are the virtually complete circuits of Conway and Caernarvon and because they are such prime examples any general survey must begin with them.

The walls of Conway, built between 1284 and 1287, form part of a larger defence scheme, the main element of which was the great, eight-towered castle described earlier in this chapter. The walls, 24 ft high and 6 ft thick, are roughly triangular in plan with a circuit, virtually complete, of about fourth-fifths of a mile (Pl. 66). There was an outer ditch on the southern and north-western sides, but not on the north-east where the River Conway formed the outer defence. There were twenty-one towers at intervals of about 130 ft and three double-towered gates, the Mill Gate on the south, the Upper Gate near the western end of the triangle, and

66   Conway town walls.

the Lower Gate on the river-front. The
southern wall was linked to the castle at
its south-west corner and the north-eastern
wall to the north-west tower of the inner
bailey, leaving the latter effectively outside
the town defences with its own separate
entrance, so that it could survive
independently of the outer bailey or the
town as a whole.

The walls of Caernarvon (built
c. 1283–6) are linked to the castle there in
very much the same way as at Conway.
The circuit, roughly D-shaped in plan, is
however much shorter, being less than half
a mile, and there are only two gates and
eight towers, at intervals of about 150–200
ft. The walls are up to 28 ft high with the
towers about 10 ft higher (Pl. 67). The
King's Gate gave access to the castle from

within the town walls but the outer bailey
had an entrance (the Queen's Gate)
beyond the walls, and there was a smaller
entrance, via the great Eagle Tower, to
the inner bailey by means of the Water
Gate, also beyond the walls.

Other originally walled towns in North
Wales include Denbigh, Rhuddlan and
Beaumaris. There are substantial remains
at Denbigh including the Burgess Gate
and the Goblin Tower, slight remains at
Rhuddlan, where the defences were of
earth and timber anyway, and virtually
nothing at Beaumaris. In mid Wales there
are no remains of the Edwardian defences
at Aberystwyth and only earthwork
remains (the stones have been robbed) at
Montgomery. In South Wales there are
good visible, but by no means complete,

67   The town walls, Caernarvon.

remains at Tenby and Pembroke.

In England the outstanding town walls are at York and Chester, with less complete but still substantial remains at Canterbury, Southampton, Oxford, Norwich, Yarmouth and Newcastle. In addition to these there are sites where the principal remains are a gateway, surviving no doubt because it was a more substantial, and often more useful, structure than the rest of the town defences. Such sites include Rye, Winchelsea, King's Lynn, Hartlepool, Warkworth, Alnwick and Beverley.

At its greatest extent the town wall of York was over three miles long, although there are now two main sections, each c. 400–500 yd in extent, where no defences survive. Until the thirteenth century the walls were of earth and timber, although

the gates may have been stone-built from the previous century. All four gates (Monk's Bar, Bootham Bar, Micklegate Bar and Walmgate Bar) were reconditioned in the time of Edward III (1327–77) and their present appearance dates from that period, except that the barbicans or outer gates of three of them were removed in the nineteenth century. The surviving barbican (Walmgate Bar) is a splendid example of the type. The walls follow the line of the Roman legionary fortress on the north and west, although little of Roman work seems to have been reused except for the Multangular Tower which formed the original south-west corner of the Roman circuit. On the south and east, however, the walls take in an additional area three or four times greater than the area of the fortress. Much of the

68   Chester: the north wall.

69   King Charles' Tower, Chester.

70 The West Gate, Canterbury, Kent.

71 Southampton: the Bargate

surviving wall stands on a substantial mound or rampart and in many places the frontal ditch, although obviously partly filled, is still very apparent.

At Chester the circuit is shorter (under two miles) but it is virtually complete, although much altered and repaired, and none of the original gates survive. On the north and east the medieval walls follow the line of the legionary fortress (Pl. 68) and on the north make use of original Roman work, in one section to a height of some 17 ft, between King Charles' Tower and the Northgate. Apart from the wall itself the principal remains are the tower just referred to and the Water Tower. King Charles' Tower (some 70 ft high) stands at the north-east angle of both the medieval walls and the original Roman fortress (Pl. 69). Although originally built in the late thirteenth or early fourteenth century the tower was almost entirely rebuilt in the seventeenth century after considerable damage suffered in the Civil War. The Water Tower (also c. 70 ft high) stands at the end of a short spur wall at the north-west corner of the medieval defences, and was part of the defences of the harbour, now Chester racecourse. The original, twin-towered medieval gateways were all replaced at various dates in the eighteenth and nineteenth centuries by the existing archway type entrances which allowed for easier movement of traffic.

Remains of town walls at other sites are less extensive but no less interesting. The existing walls at Canterbury belong to the late fourteenth and early fifteenth century, although they are a rebuilding or replacement of an earlier system. The most notable feature is the double-towered West Gate (Pl. 70). The best preserved sections of wall (with semi-circular towers) are on the eastern side of the city where they are backed by a great earth rampart. At Southampton about half of the original circuit of just over a mile has survived, including thirteen towers (of an original twenty-nine), and four gates (out of

seven), of which the most impressive is the Bargate, as much a monument to civic pride as to defence (Pl. 71). Other sites with visible remains of walls include Newcastle-on-Tyne, Norwich, Oxford and Yarmouth. At a number of other places the principal remnant of the town defences is a gatehouse. These have probably survived because the accommodation above the gateway was useful for domestic or business purposes. Well-preserved town gates exist at Rye, Winchelsea, King's Lynn, Beverley, Hartlepool, Alnwick and Warkworth.

5 Tower-houses

Tower-houses have been mentioned already in connection with fourteenth- and fifteenth-century additions to existing English castles (pp. 126–33). The same term, however, embraces a much greater range of fortifications in Scotland and Ireland where such towers, rather than forming part of a larger complex, stand alone with only a small stone-walled courtyard or barmkin on one side, at least in their original state; in many cases there are, of course, structural additions of later periods, of which the tower forms the nucleus. In the same category are the numerous 'pele-towers' of northern England (mainly Northumberland and Cumbria), although there are differing uses of the term pele which can cause misunderstanding. For Brian Long (*Castles of Northumberland*, 1967, p. 16) a pele is a building with a vaulted basement (for livestock), with family accommodation on the first floor, reached by an outside staircase. Description and illustration, however, make it quite clear that these are the structures described by the Royal Commission on Historical Monuments as 'bastles' (below, p. 147), which can be briefly described as fortified farmhouses. They have pitched roofs and are certainly not tower-like in appearance. The most generally accepted definition of a pele is that of a fortified residence in the form of a tower, and as such the basic concept is very much the same as that of the Scottish and Irish tower-houses. For this reason pele-towers, tower-houses in Scotland and tower-houses in Ireland will be treated as three related groups under the general chapter heading of tower-houses.

Northern Tower-houses

For about three centuries, from the time of Edward I (1272–1307) until the union of England and Scotland in 1603, the northern counties of England were very much a frontier zone, as in Roman times. The constant threat of Scottish raids or larger scale incursions led to the building of domestic accommodation in the form of towers, manor houses up-ended as described earlier (p. 127). Their social status, as implied by the term manor house, needs to be emphasized. These are not the great royal or baronial castles of Chapters 3 and 4. They are much humbler structures of only local importance, as indeed their numbers indicate. In Cumbria, Northumberland and adjacent areas there are remains of some 200 such towers, in addition to, rather than instead of, the great castles. These towers are in effect the local manor houses of the northern counties, built in a form made necessary by local conditions during the fourteenth, fifteenth and sixteenth centuries.

72 Arnside Tower, Cumbria.

Sizergh Castle (Cumbria), just south of Kendal, is an excellent example of one of these northern towers with, as in many other cases, additions of later periods. The tower, built *c.* 1350, measures 60 × 40 ft in plan and stands some 58 ft high, with a small turret rising 10 ft higher. The walls of the vaulted basement are up to 9 ft thick and there are three storeys above. As first built this tower stood alone, probably surrounded by a wet moat, but there have been considerable additions over the centuries and the whole complex now surrounds three sides of a courtyard. The earliest addition, as in a number of other cases, seems to have been a great hall, of *c.* 1450, which would, no doubt, have provided greater domestic comfort in peaceful interludes with the adjacent tower still available in times of trouble.

Unlike Sizergh there are no structures other than the original tower at either Arnside or Dalton. Arnside, built *c.* 1330, now stands gaunt and isolated on a small hillock a mile or so outside the village (Pl. 72). One half of the structure has fallen away. The tower, *c.* 50 ft high, was 45 × 31 ft in plan, with a large turret, *c.* 13 × 12 ft at the north-west corner. Dalton Tower, in the village of Dalton-in-Furness, is intact, although much altered. It was built about the same time as Arnside and measured 45 × 30 ft in plan. Shank Castle, near Stapleton (Cumbria), is in a similar state to Arnside. It is 52 × 29 ft in plan and was originally *c.* 45 ft high.

Many of the best preserved towers form part of a larger and later complex, in

143

73 Dacre Castle, Cumbria

some cases still occupied, as at Sizergh, and this, indeed, is the reason for their survival. Yanwath Hall (Cumbria) is such a site. The tower ($38 \times 30 \times 55$ ft high) was built early in the fourteenth century. It has a vaulted basement, two storeys above that and four corner turrets rising above the battlemented parapet. In the following century a great hall and kitchen range were added to the east side of the tower, and subsequent additions enclosed a courtyard on three sides. Other Cumbrian sites in this category include: Catterlen Hall, with a fifteenth-century tower, and extensive additions enclosing a courtyard, and Askham Hall, with an original fourteenth-century tower, given new windows,

c. 1685–90, and with the battlements restored in Victorian times. Other well-preserved Cumbrian towers include Dacre Castle (early fourteenth century), with large square towers at two opposite corners and two smaller, buttress-like towers at the two remaining corners (Pl. 73), Strickland's Tower (fourteenth century) in Rose Castle, and Dacre's Tower (fourteenth century) in Naworth Castle.

Remains in Northumberland are equally varied and impressive. As in Cumbria many of the best preserved examples are incorporated in later buildings, of several periods, and a number are still occupied. An excellent

74 Chipchase Tower, Northumberland.

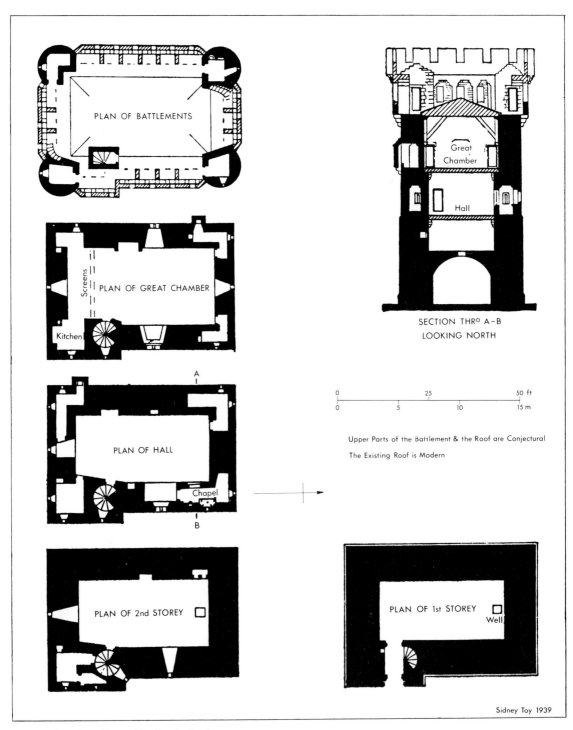

PLAN OF BATTLEMENTS

Great
Chamber

Hall

SECTION THRº A–B
LOOKING NORTH

Screens
PLAN OF GREAT CHAMBER

Kitchen

0		25		50 ft
0	5	10		15 m

Upper Parts of the Battlement & the Roof are Conjectural

The Existing Roof is Modern

A

PLAN OF HALL

Chapel

B

PLAN OF 2nd STOREY

PLAN OF 1st STOREY

Well

Sidney Toy 1939

Fig. 25   Chipchase Tower, Northumberland.

example of an early house (*c.* 1300), unencumbered by later buildings, is provided by the Vicar's Pele in Corbridge, standing on the south side of the churchyard. As its name implies it was simply the vicar's house, built as a matter of course in the tower style because of the troublesome conditions. Vicar's Pele is a simple rectangular tower, *c.* 27 × 21 × 40 ft high with the usual vaulted basement and two floors above. Small square turrets, carried on corbels, projected from each corner. Apart from these and the battlemented parapet the exterior of the tower is quite plain, with only a ground floor doorway and a few window slits. Vicars' houses of generally similar form are known also at Alnham, Elsdon, Embleton, Ford, Ponteland and Whitton.

Chipchase Tower, slightly later than Corbridge but still of the fourteenth century, now forms part of a magnificent mansion added in Jacobean times (*c.* 1621). It is also much larger than Corbridge, 51 × 34 × 50 ft high, with another 10 ft for the original height of the four angle turrets which in this case are circular (Pl. 74). There is the usual vaulted basement with three further floors above (Fig. 25). There is a shallow wing at the south end of the east wall, accommodating the spiral staircase and an additional small room on each floor, one of them forming the kitchen. At Belsay Castle (*c.* 1340) there are two such wings, one at each end of the west side, providing two additional rooms on each floor (Pl. 75). The basement (kitchen) was vaulted and there were two floors above, one containing the great hall and the one above the great chamber or private apartments of the owner.

Rather more spectacular, in both scale and appearance, are Langley Castle and Haughton Castle, both of the fourteenth century. Langley's impressive exterior is due in part to late nineteenth- and early twentieth-century restoration, but this appears to have been faithful to the original appearance. The tower consists of an oblong centre block, forming one main room on each floor, and four large rectangular corner towers, containing four additional rooms on each floor. Haughton Castle is also oblong in plan, with four corner towers flush with the main walls. It is large by northern tower-house standards (107 × 49 ft) and this seems to have been the result, at least in part, of creating a tower-house by adapting an existing house, rather than by building anew as in most other cases. Other Northumbrian towers worth noting are Halton Tower, Featherstone Castle, Cocklaw Tower, and the Moot Hall and the Prison at Hexham, both of the northern tower-house type in spite of their names.

Although the majority of tower-houses are to be found in Cumbria and Northumberland, there are also a few in Lancashire, not only in the northern part of the county, at Borwick Hall, for example, but also much further south, at Turton Tower (Pl. 76), recently restored, just north of Bolton, and Radcliffe Tower, now in ruins, between Bolton and Manchester.

The term 'bastle' has been referred to already (p. 142). The Royal Commission on Historical Monuments (England) define a bastle as a 'small fortified farmhouse, with accommodation for human beings on the upper floor and for livestock below' (*Shielings and Bastles*, 1970, p. xiv). This type of structure may well have been the result of deliberate policy relating to the border zone. Some seventy or eighty bastles survive (out of an original total of several hundred), and virtually all of them are confined to a zone some 20 miles wide along the border. They are, moreover, fairly closely dated to the late sixteenth and first half of the seventeenth centuries. By this time the power of the feudal lords, who had looked to the defence of the border, was at an end, largely as a result of the much more centralized government of the Tudor monarchs. With them had gone many of the longstanding border castles and towers.

75   Belsay Tower, Northumberland.

76 Turton Tower, Bolton, Lancashire.

Defence, originally in the hands of the great barons, later in those of the lords of the manor, now devolved in turn upon smaller landowners and farmers who provided themselves with fortified farmhouses which we call bastles. The idea was not so much to defend themselves against a Scottish army (for which they would have been useless), as against sporadic raiding by small armed bands intent on cattle raiding and looting. By about 1650 or 1660 other, unfortified, types of houses were being built in the bastle area, so that presumably the need for this type of fortification was at an end, although, of course, existing bastles continued to be used simply as farmhouses.

In construction the bastle clearly owes something to the tower-house. Its ground floor is normally tunnel-vaulted and this was certainly used for cattle in later times and was probably the original purpose as well. The major difference from the tower-house was in plan and elevation. In plan the bastle was oblong, up to 40 ft long (and occasionally longer), and about 20 ft wide, with walls c. 4 ft thick. Its domestic accommodation was at first floor level and the building rose no higher than this except, in some cases, for a small attic contrived in the roof space; the roof was of the gabled type. Access to the living quarters was by means of an outside staircase, in surviving examples of stone, but originally in the form of a wooden ladder which could be drawn up in time of danger. Internal communication between upper and lower floors was by means of a trap door and ladder or, in

77　Etal Tower and gatehouse, Northumberland.

some cases, by a narrow stair. Of the seventy or eighty surviving bastles a number are upstanding ruins, but many are still in use, serving a variety of purposes on present-day working farms.

Tower-houses in Scotland

In England the tower-house is a localized, regional type, made necessary by peculiar circumstances in the northern counties in the years 1300–1600. In Scotland, however, in whatever circumstances it began, the tower-house came to be the universal type, found throughout the country from the border to Shetland and from the east coast to the Western Isles.

The close relationship between Scottish tower-houses and those of northern England can be gauged from one site,

Elphinstone Tower (Lothian). For Stuart Cruden (*The Scottish Castle*, 1960, p. 136) Elphinstone is a thoroughgoing Scottish tower-house. Sidney Toy, however, treats it as a pele-tower, to be distinguished, if only on grounds of date, from the main run of border towers (*The Castles of Great Britain*, 1953, p. 201). The fact is that any such distinction is virtually meaningless. Towers were built in large numbers on both sides of the Scottish border for about 300 years (1300–1600). Differences which exist are differences of detail; fundamentally they are all of the same basic type, a house, socially at the manor house level, built in the form of a tower. Elphinstone belongs just as much with the tower-houses of Scotland as it does with Sizergh Castle or Vicar's Pele, Corbridge, because ultimately all such towers form a single typological group.

Elphinstone (built *c.* 1440) is by no means among the earliest Scottish tower-houses although it does retain the simple rectangular layout at a time when other plans, most notably the simple L-plan, were being employed (Fig. 27, a). Among well-preserved examples of early (i.e. late thirteenth and fourteenth century) rectangular tower-houses are Threave (Dumfries & Galloway), Drum (Grampian), Cawdor (Highland county) and Crichton (Lothian); with the exception of Threave all have been added to in later centuries.

The tower-house at Threave measures 60×40 ft in plan and still stands to nearly its original height of *c.* 70 ft (Pl. 78). The accommodation is divided into five storeys. Entry was at first floor (second storey) level where the kitchen was situated, with access to the basement below probably by means of a trap door. The third storey housed the great hall with additional, more private, accommodation on the fourth

storey. The topmost storey probably housed the military part of the household. The tower is surrounded by a rectangular curtain wall of the following (fifteenth) century, pierced by gun-ports rather than arrow slits, one of the earliest examples of artillery defence in Scotland.

Drum near Aberdeen is of similar dimensions ($53 \times 40 \times 70$ ft high) and is virtually intact, although subsequently a house was added to it in the seventeenth century. The corners are rounded and the exterior is otherwise quite plain, except for the battlements at the top. Internally, like Threave, it is of five storeys with access to the basement storey from above (first floor level) where the main entrance was situated. Cawdor Tower is somewhat smaller than the other two (*c.* 45×44 ft) and was originally of only four storeys, although a roof chamber was added in the seventeenth century. There were considerable additions and alterations in the fifteenth, sixteenth and seventeenth

Fig. 26 Elphinstone Tower, Lothian.

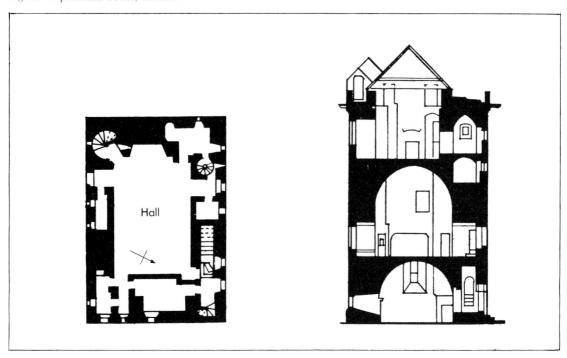

78 Threave Castle, Dumfries & Galloway.

centuries, producing the existing plan with ranges of buildings and courtyards on all sides, the whole surrounded by a moat on three sides (crossed by a drawbridge), and a stream on the fourth. The tower-house at Crichton was added to in a similar way, although only one courtyard was involved there. The original tower is of similar dimensions to Cawdor (46 × 33 ft). The vaulted basement, at ground floor level, was entered directly from the outside; access to the first floor hall was by means of an external stair. There was no direct communication between the basement and the hall above.

Such towers as these were basically simple both in plan (a rectangle) and internal arrangement (a single room on each floor). Inevitably, in the remaining portion of the fourteenth century and in

the fifteenth century, there were developments, within the basic tower formula, to provide additional and more varied accommodation. One way of doing this was to make use of the thickness of the walls above ground floor level, as at Elphinstone Tower (Lothian), mentioned earlier. Elphinstone (built c. 1440) retains the simple rectangular plan (50 × 35 ft), but within the thickness of its walls, in addition to the main room on each floor, there is a whole series of smaller chambers which must have added greatly to its comfort and convenience. The tower, 70 ft high, is divided into five storeys, two of them, including the great hall, vaulted. Entry was at ground floor level and a straight staircase in the thickness of the wall led up to the great hall. The tower-house at Comlongon (Dumfries &

Galloway) is of similar date and plan to Elphinstone, with the same multiplicity of rooms contrived in the thickness of the wall.

The alternative method of providing additional accommodation was to build an L-shaped rather than a simple rectangular tower (Fig. 27, b). An early example (*c.* 1374) is Craigmillar Castle (Edinburgh), which is simply a rectangular tower (52 × 38 ft) with an additional tower or wing (*c.* 30 × 10 ft) added to one of the long sides, forming a squat L-shape in plan (Pl. 79). This allowed at least some of the rooms to be alongside each other rather than superimposed, for example, the great hall and the kitchen or the great hall and the solar (i.e. a private apartment). The L-shaped tower at Craigmillar originally stood alone, but in the fifteenth century an outer curtain wall was added and this is probably the earliest artillery fortification in Scotland, even earlier than Threave (above, p. 151). The tower is preserved virtually to its full height although it lacks a roof and there are substantial remains of the buildings added in the following centuries.

There are many other towers built on the L-shaped plan in the fourteenth and fifteenth centuries. Glamis Castle (Tayside), now a large and complex structure, much added to and rebuilt in

79 Craigmillar Castle, Edinburgh.

later centuries, almost certainly contains an original nucleus in the form of an L-shaped tower of the late fourteenth century. The additional wing is larger than Craigmillar (c. 30 × 20 ft), while the one at Dunottar (Grampian), also of the late fourteenth century is smaller (c. 20 × 16 ft). In the following century the one at Affleck (Tayside) is smaller again (12 × 6 ft), although both it and Dunottar are attached to relatively small main towers, both c. 37 × 20 ft only. Dundas (Lothian) is a fifteenth-century example of the L-plan to which a second wing or tower was added later in an attempt to increase the accommodation.

The majority of Scottish tower-houses of the fourteenth and fifteenth centuries conform to the simple rectangular or L-shaped plan, although, as just indicated, a second tower or wing could be sometimes added to the latter. There are, however, a few examples in the same period of tower-houses built on a more elaborate plan. One of the best preserved is Borthwick Castle (Lothian), built c. 1430 (Fig. 27, c). This consists, in plan, of a main tower with two additional wings, both on the same, west side, all rising to the same height, nearly 100 ft overall. The main tower is 75 × 47 ft in area and the additional wings, c. 30 × 20 ft each, which, even allowing for the great thickness of the walls (c. 12 ft), still provides a great deal of accommodation on each floor. The main entrance was at first floor level and was reached, via a drawbridge, from the rampart walk of the surrounding curtain wall. At this level was the great hall (c. 50 × 24 ft), with the kitchen occupying one wing and the solar or private apartment the other, together with additional small rooms and staircases contrived in the thickness of the walls. There is a vaulted basement forming the first storey and three further storeys above the great hall and its associated rooms. The tower-house stands within a curtain wall designed for artillery which was added c. 1500.

Even more elaborate in plan was Hermitage Castle (Borders), a large tower-house originally built as a manor house c. 1360 (Fig. 27, h). This was converted to a rectangular tower-house late in the century and shortly afterwards four corner towers were added (c. 1400), giving the Hermitage its present striking appearance (Pl. 80). The main central tower measures 75 × 45 ft. The additional towers mask the four angles and are all of different sizes, the smallest, at the north-east, being c. 23 ft square, the largest, at the south-west, being c. 56 × 32 ft, which is by itself larger than some free-standing tower-houses. At the eastern and western ends the gaps between the towers are bridged across at fourth storey level. There is a generally similar tower-house with four corner towers at Crookston (Strathclyde) and another is known (from excavation) at Braemar (Grampian), the castle of Kindrochit. The main tower blocks at Borthwick and the Hermitage are very similar in size. The difference lies in the way in which additional accommodation was provided. At Borthwick two additional towers or wings were built on one face of the main tower, while at the Hermitage, Crookston and Braemar, four towers were provided at the angles, dominating the external elevations and almost concealing the existence of the central block.

Tower-houses of the types just described (rectangular and L-shaped, plus the few more elaborate plans), were the rule during the first half of the three-century period of tower-house building mentioned earlier, that is, from about 1330 to about 1480. After 1480 there was a noticeable slowing down in activity for about eighty years. Although a few tower-houses were built during this time, to a large extent the demand for this type of accommodation had by then been largely met by the fairly intensive activity of the previous century and a half. There were, in addition, social and political reasons for the slackening of effort and interest in

80   Hermitage Castle, Borders.

tower-house building during the ensuing
eighty or so years. This pause ended with
the return of Mary Queen of Scots from
France in 1561, and within a few years
another great period of tower-house
building was under way. In England this
was the era in which the great
Elizabethan houses were being built.
There were no such houses in Scotland.
Instead, there was a resumption of tower-
house building, but now on a much more
ambitious scale, including many which are
deservedly well known and in most cases
still occupied. This second phase of tower-
house building in Scotland lasted about a
century or more, from *c.* 1560–1670,
although in the last few decades tower-
houses were being superseded by purely
domestic, non-Scottish types of house, with

no pretensions to military strength and
security.

Although totally different in external
appearance from the great Elizabethan
country houses, the Scottish tower-houses
of this second phase had in common with
them the desire to provide more spacious
accommodation than had been possible in
the older towers, except for the larger
examples such as Borthwick and
Hermitage Castle which, in a sense,
pointed the way in which the simple
rectangular tower could develop. Without
completely abandoning the tower idea the
only feasible way to extend the
accommodation in the direction of
convenience was to mutiply the number of
towers on a much more elaborate scale
than the simple squat L-plan, or even the

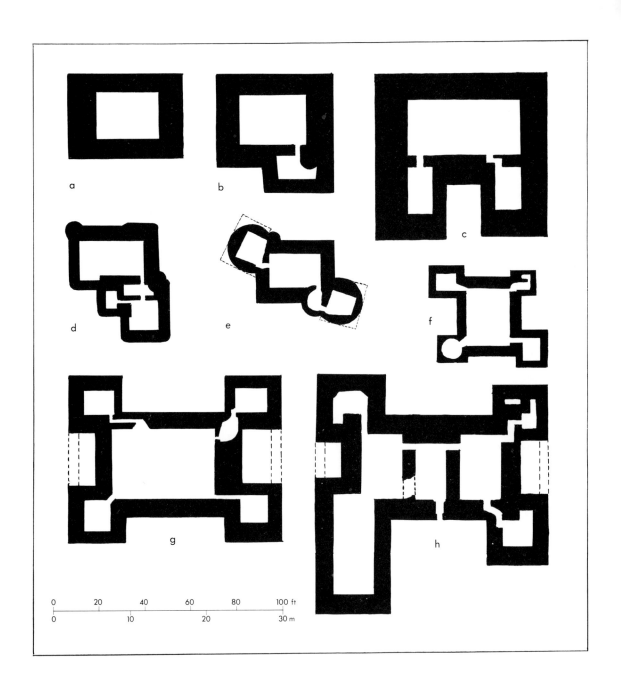

Fig. 27   Outline plans of Scottish and Irish tower-houses:
(a) Elphinstone Tower, Lothian; (b) Craigmillar,
Lothian;   (c)   Borthwick,   Lothian;   (d)   Craigievar,
Grampian; (e) Claypotts, Tayside; (f) Dunsoghley, Co.
Dublin; (g) Bunratty, Co. Clare; (h) Hermitage Castle,
Borders.

more ambitious Borthwick or Hermitage plans, and this, in fact, was the basis on which virtually all the later tower-houses were planned.

Following this principle two basic plans developed which became virtually standard types: the so called L-plan and the so called Z-plan (Fig. 27, d, e). Although other methods of increasing accommodation were occasionally tried (e.g. adding to the height or to the ground plan of the basic rectangular towers), these were very much in a minority as compared with the two methods mentioned above. Increasing the height and number of floors upheld the tower principle but the result was still very inconvenient. Increasing the rectangular base area of the tower made for convenience but because of the changed proportions the effect of a tower was lost. Quite clearly convenience and appearance needed to go hand in hand, and in the L- and Z-plans this combination was satisfactorily achieved.

The L-plan, albeit in simple form, was well established in the early period of tower-house building (1330-1480). The Z-plan, however (Fig. 27, e), is known mainly from the later period (after 1560), although there is at least one example which appears to be earlier. Huntly Castle (Grampian) was built on the foundations of an earlier castle of *c.* 1450 which anticipates the numerous Z-plan tower-houses of the later period. It has a central rectangular tower block (*c.* 80 × 40 ft) with towers at two diagonally opposite corners and this is the basis of the Z-plan. In fact, in this case, the (round) towers are very unevenly matched, one being very large, *c.* 40 ft in diameter, the other being simply a small stair tower *c.* 15 ft in diameter. Nevertheless, Huntly contains the three basic elements of the Z-plan: a rectangular main tower block, with two additional towers, either round or rectangular, at two diagonally opposite corners. In terms of convenience the advantages are obvious: groups of rooms

can now be placed *en suite* instead of being stacked up vertically. In terms of appearance the three structural elements can be seen as virtually three separate towers, so that the tower-house aspect is still very strikingly acknowledged.

In spite of Huntly Castle, however, it remains true that for all practical purposes the Z-plan is a feature of post-1560 tower-houses. Within this period one of the earliest, and in many ways the most striking examples is Claypotts (Tayside) built in 1569 (Fig. 27, e). It consists of a main rectangular tower (*c.* 33 × 22 ft), with circular towers (diameter 20 ft) at the north-eastern and south-western angles, thus conforming to the Z formula. Although the corner towers are circular at the base and remain so through the first four storeys, in their uppermost sections they are rectangular, and it is this feature in both towers which gives Claypotts much of its striking appearance. The great projection of the towers meant that all four faces of the main tower could be protected by gunfire and gun-ports for defence were provided in both towers at ground floor level.

The circular corner towers at Drochil (Borders), built *c.* 1581, also have rectangular upper portions, as at Claypotts. The towers are larger (27 ft in diameter) but they are dwarfed by the enormous main block to which they are attached which is nearly 85 × 70 ft in plan. Midmar (Grampian) is of more normal dimensions (main tower 28 × 26 ft), with a circular tower at the south-east angle and a rectangular one at the north-west. At Castle Menzies (Tayside), on the other hand (built 1571-7), both corner towers of the Z-plan are rectangular and are as big as many a free-standing tower (Pl. 81). There are gun-ports at ground floor level and decorated dormer windows, stepped gables and corner turrets at the upper level. Glamis Castle (mentioned earlier, p. 153) also belongs, by the early seventeenth century, to the Z-plan category. The diagonally opposite rectangular corner

81 Castle Menzies, Tayside.

towers were certainly built then and the main central tower may have been rebuilt at the same time; if not, it was almost certainly refurbished in line with prevailing tower-house fashion.

The oustanding example of the L-plan, and probably the most picturesque tower-house in Scotland, is Craigievar (Grampian). It is, in fact, as in many other L-plan tower-houses of the late period, of the stepped L-type, there being a third, small tower in the angle between the two main towers (Fig. 27, d). Built in 1626 it has retained most, if not all, of its original appearance, and is still occupied. In spite of its plan, the most striking aspect of Craigievar is its elevation with its

rounded corners, plain lower walls and elaborate corner turrets with conical roofs rising over 70 ft high. Craigievar is, in many ways, the epitome of the whole tower-house building concept. It is so essentially a simple tower, in spite of its stepped L-plan; it is also very much a house, in spite of the military, tower form. Another L-shaped house, Crathes (also in Grampian), is not dissimilar in general appearance but the overall effect is not quite so successful as Craigievar (Pl. 82). Barcaldine Castle (Strathclyde, early seventeenth century) can also be classed as of the stepped L-type, although the tower in the re-entrant angle is round rather than rectangular. The main tower is 47 × 30 ft,

82 Crathes Castle, Grampian.

83 Castle Tirrim, Moidart.

the adjacent tower 25 ft square and the circular tower *c.* 17 ft in diameter. Dunskey Castle (Dumfries & Galloway) has a double step in the re-entrant angle and one arm of the L-plan is much longer than usual, *c.* 90 ft. Maclellans House (Dumfries & Galloway) also has the double step arrangement in the re-entrant angle and there is an additional rectangular tower at the opposite, outside angle.

One or two other sites quite clearly belong with the L- and Z-plan tower-houses although they are not clear cut examples of either. Earlshall (Fife) has a stepped L-plan but it also has, on the diagonally opposite corner of the main tower (59 × 27½ ft), an oval tower, giving it something of a Z-plan appearance. Castle Kennedy (Dumfries & Galloway), of the early seventeenth century, also belongs to the stepped L-plan group, although it has two such arrangements, one on each side of the main tower. Elcho (Tayside) likewise has a double L-plan arrangement (one stepped, one plain), but it has, in addition, two circular towers, one at the opposite angle to the L-plan arrangement, forming a Z-plan, and one midway between it and the stepped L. Viewed

160

from the south-east Elcho looks like an ordinary **Z**-plan tower-house, similar in general appearance to Castle Menzies (above, p. 157) except for the shape of one of the corner towers. Nisbet House (Borders, early seventeenth century) also has four towers disposed around the main tower block (63×21 ft). There are two round towers at opposite ends of one of the long sides and two rectangular towers on the other long side, one at the corner and one, smaller, midway along the visible face of the main tower. Craigook Castle (Lothian) is a simpler version of this. It has a main tower block (60×22 ft), with one circular corner tower and one rectangular tower midway along the opposite long side.

In addition to the **L**- and **Z**-plan towers and their variants just noted, one or two other examples of late tower-houses need to be noted to complete the picture. The simple rectangular tower was not entirely superseded by more elaborate plans. At Amisfield (Dumfries & Galloway), built as late as 1600, the answer to the need for greater accommodation was the one mentioned earlier, that of increasing the height of the tower and therefore the number of floors. In spite of its height (*c.* 90 ft), Amisfield is only 30×30 ft in area, so that however many extra rooms the additional floors provided they could never be conveniently grouped together *en suite*. Communication was still exclusively vertical. Coxton (Grampian), even later in date (1644), likewise retains the simple rectangular plan of earlier times.

At the opposite end of the scale is Fyvie (Grampian), a palatial tower-house complex, built *c.* 1600. This is the only example of its kind but it does demonstrate very forcefully the strength of the tower-house tradition. It consists, in effect, of three tower-houses in a line linked by two lower, linking ranges, the whole providing an impressive façade some 150 ft in length. For once the vertical

84 Doune Castle, Tayside.

85   Clara Castle, Kilkenny.

aspect (five storeys, 65 ft) is less than the horizontal, but because it consists of three linked towers rather than a single structure, the effect is not lost and there is no doubt that Fyvie is part of the tower-house tradition, even if a very particular part.

Tower-houses in Ireland

Until the early decades of the fourteenth century Irish fortifications were very much on the same lines as those in England and Wales, as indicated earlier (pp. 84–106). After about 1320, however, there was a noticeable pause in building activity which lasted until well into the following century. By about 1450 a massive revival of building, both religious and secular, was under way, and this included very large numbers of tower-houses which, as in Scotland, dominated the domestic scene. The tower-house period in Ireland was somewhat shorter than in Scotland, around two centuries (*c.* 1450–1650), but the results, in terms of numbers built and surviving visible remains, are no less impressive. Although no precise figures are available tower-houses in Ireland must be counted in thousands, with particular

Fig. 28   Clara Castle, Co. Kilkenny.

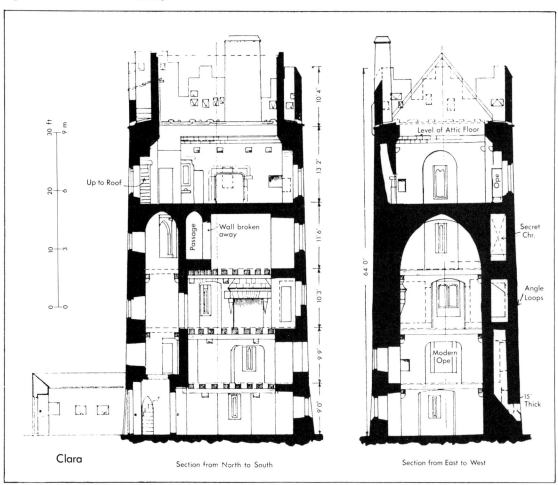

concentrations in Clare, Cork, Galway, Kilkenny, Limerick and Tipperary.

Although there are points of difference between the tower-houses of Ireland and those of Scotland, these are more than outweighed by the very considerable resemblances between the two groups which make it quite clear that they are essentially the same type of construction, in essence a manor house with the accommodation extending vertically rather than horizontally, for reasons of security. As in Scotland, the basic type is the simple rectangular tower. Clara Castle in Kilkenny is a well-preserved example of the type (Pl. 85). It was built late in the fifteenth century on a rectangular plan,

$c. 34 \times 27$ ft and rose (through five storeys plus an attic), to an overall height of 70 ft (Fig. 28). It has a walled courtyard or bawn in front of the entrance, which is at ground level. The fifth storey floor is supported by a stone vault, the rest by (still surviving) oak beams on stone corbels. The crenellations at the top of the tower are in the Irish fashion, that is the merlons are stepped on each side; in this case there are two steps, but in other cases there are three, producing a touch of greater elegance than the more rugged simple rectangular merlon could provide. Some of the crenellations at Burnchurch Castle in the same county are of the three-stepped type. Burnchurch is broadly

86 Burnchurch Castle and Tower, Kilkenny.

87   Derryhivenny Castle, Co. Galway.

similar in size and layout to Clara but differs in one respect. The gable-end walls are carried up one storey higher than the other two walls and are, in effect, two elongated turrets with their own rampart walks at the highest part of the building (Pl. 86). Derryhivenny (Galway), built in 1643, is another well-preserved rectangular tower-house, distinguished by a largely surviving L-shaped courtyard or bawn, with two round corner towers, which covers two sides of the tower (Pl. 87).

Included in the towers of simple rectangular plan are many of the so called 'ten-pound' castles, built as the result of a statute of Henry VI in 1429. This was designed to encourage the building of tower-houses in the counties of Dublin, Meath, Kildare and Louth (the counties of the English pale) by offering a subsidy of ten pounds for each tower built. Minimum dimensions were laid down ($20 \times 16 \times 40$ ft high), noticeably less than the dimensions of the three towers considered above. A tower-house at Donore (Meath) conforms closely to the specification. It was $c. 28 \times 22$ ft in plan with rounded corners and a stair turret in one corner (Pl. 88). It was of four storeys, the lower two covered by a stone vault. Presumably the offer of a subsidy was successful, for in 1449, only twenty years

88　Donore Castle, near Killyon, Co. Meath.

89   Blarney Castle, Co. Cork.

later, a limitation was imposed on the numbers to be built. However, it seems probable that many of the smaller rectangular towers in these four counties around Dublin were the result of the statute of 1429 and the ten pound subsidy.

Although there are tower-houses in Ireland which go beyond the straightforward rectangular plan, there is nothing to match the large and elaborate towers of the second period of Scottish building (1560–1670). By and large, the resemblances are with the earlier Scottish period (1330–1480). The simplest addition to the rectangular plan was, as in Scotland, the provision of a second,

smaller tower, alongside the first, producing a squat, L-shaped plan. Probably the best known example of this type is Blarney Castle (Co. Cork), built c. 1446, famous for its Blarney Stone (Pl. 89). The main tower is massive, 85 ft high overall, with walls 12 ft thick in the lower part of the structure. There are two storeys in this section, surmounted by a stone vault, and three storeys above with timber floors. The tower, which tapers slightly, is surmounted by double-stepped Irish crenellations. Abutting one side and projecting beyond the angle is a much smaller, somewhat lower, tower containing a staircase and some smaller rooms. At

90 Roodstown Castle, Co. Louth.

91   Bunratty Castle, Co. Clare.

Roodstown (Co. Louth) the staircase is housed in the same way, leaving space in the main tower for a single, uncluttered rectangular room (*c.* 13 × 16 ft). There is a second, smaller tower or jamb at the diagonally opposite corner (*c.* 7 × 3 ft). The tower is of four storeys, 23 ft square in plan (not counting the two subsidiary towers), and *c.* 45 ft high, and was probably one of the ten-pound castles mentioned above, built in the fifteenth century (Pl. 90).

As in Scotland even in the earlier period there are one or two more ambitious plans. Kilclief (Co. Down) has two additional towers projecting from one face of the main tower, the same arrangement as noted earlier at Borthwick in Lothian (p. 154). The space between the towers is spanned by an arch at fourth storey level, in the same way as the towers at Hermitage Castle (Borders) (above, p. 154). Bunratty Castle (Co. Clare), one of the finest in Ireland, shows even greater resemblance to the same site (Fig. 27, g). It consists of a main tower (*c.* 64 × 43 ft), with four rectangular flanking towers, one marking each angle, with arches spanning the gaps high up on the north and south sides (Pl. 91). The main block is of three storeys, the corner towers of six storeys each. Dunsoghley (Co. Dublin) is another site with four angle towers, although on a smaller scale (Pl. 92). The main block

92   Dunsoghley Castle, Co. Dublin.

93 Ballynahow Castle, Tipperary.

94 Lohort Castle, Co. Cork.

95　Donegal Castle, Co. Donegal.

($c. 33 \times 28$ ft) is surrounded by four corner
towers which vary in size. Two at
diagonally opposite angles are $c.$ 11 ft
square while the two remaining towers are
13×14 ft and 14×15 ft (Fig. 27, f).

The more ambitious Irish towers
include also an example of the so called Z-
plan (above, p. 157). This is Burt Castle
(Co. Donegal), built late in the sixteenth
century. It consists of a rectangular main
block ($c. 30 \times 22$ ft) with round towers (10–
12 ft in diameter) at two diagonally
opposite corners, one of them containing
the staircase. An illustration of 1601 gives
a good idea of the original appearance of
the tower with its surrounding bawn or
courtyard and an external ditch.

Circular towers in Ireland form a type
of tower-house for which there appears to
be no parallel in Scotland, although, apart
from the circular plan, such towers are
exactly the same in purpose and function
as the rectangular towers. Ballynahow
(Tipperary) has two superimposed stone
vaults, each containing two storeys, and a
fifth storey in the conical roof (Pl. 93). In
spite of the external appearance the main
rooms are more or less square. The round
tower-house at Newtown (Co. Clare) rises
from a rectangular plinth or base shaped
like the lower part of a pyramid. Another
round tower, Reginald's Tower, at
Waterford, forms part of the city walls,
but is otherwise the same as the free-

96 Monea Castle, Co. Fermanagh.

standing types. Other circular tower-houses are known at Synone (Tipperary) and Balief (Co. Kilkenny).

The numerous Irish tower-houses include the following which are substantially preserved if not, in a number of cases, virtually intact: Danganbrack, Urlanmore and Leamaneagh Castle (Co. Clare), the latter with a later, seventeenth-century house attached to one side of it; Carrigaphooca and Lohort (Co. Cork) (Pl. 94); Buncrana and Donegal Castle (Donegal), the second with a gabled house of 1610 added (Pl. 95); Dalkey village (Co. Dublin, with two tower houses in the main street); Fiddaun (Galway), a very tall tower standing in a large and well-preserved bawn or courtyard; Carrigafoyle (Co. Kerry), similar in size to Fiddaun and likewise standing originally within a walled courtyard; Granny Castle (Kilkenny); Ballygrennan (Limerick), standing at the junction of two bawns, each containing a house of later date; Athclare (Louth), a still inhabited sixteenth-century tower-house with an attached great hall, apparently of the same date; Lough Mark and Rockfleet (Mayo); Clonony (Offaly), noted for its fine bawn with crenellations and corner towers; Knockelly (Tipperary); and Coolhull and Rathmacknee (Wexford), the latter with a well-preserved bawn with a corner turret.

The late sixteenth and early seventeenth centuries saw the building of many large houses, distinguished by numerous gables and obviously built with comfort and elegance in mind. Nevertheless, these houses retained some defensive features, such as corbels high on the walls to support a gallery for defence purposes, and were often built on an elaborate tower-house plan with a central rectangular block and four rectangular tower-like blocks at the corners. During the same period thoroughgoing tower-houses were still being built and went on being built until c. 1650.

One final group of structures needs to be noted here. These are the so called plantation castles built in the north of Ireland in the early decades of the seventeenth century. They were built by English and Scottish settlers who had received grants of land as part of a settlement plan. Among the terms of the grants was the requirement to build a castle or fortified house or enclosure, and many structures were built to meet this condition. Many were simply rectangular walled bawns or courtyards with a house down one side, but one or two were more elaborate, of which the most famous is Monea Castle (Co. Fermanagh). This, in fact, consists of a tower-house standing within a bawn, although most of the latter has now gone. The tower, however, is well preserved (Pl. 96). It consists of a main rectangular tower, c. 60 × 40 × 50 ft high with two round towers masking the corners of one of the shorter sides. The whole structure is given a very Scottish appearance by the upper storeys of the corner towers which are rectangular, very much in the manner of Claypotts (above, p. 157), built only a few decades before, and there is little doubt that Monea represents the ideas of a Scottish settler in Ireland on what a defensible house should look like.

6 Artillery Fortifications

Although guns and gunpowder were introduced into warfare in the first half of the fourteenth century it was not until nearly two centuries later that fortifications specially designed for artillery were built in the British Isles. In the intervening years, for the most part, existing castles were adapted, as far as their design would allow, to the requirements of hand-held and heavier guns. For the latter, in particular, the high curtain walls and tall towers of medieval castles were quite unsuitable. It was inevitable, therefore, that in time new types of fortification would be developed to meet the needs of artillery warfare. The subject of artillery fortification is, in technical terms, a vast one and for reasons of space cannot be pursued here in any detail. As compared with earlier periods, surviving remains are comparatively scarce, and in this chapter attention will be largely confined to those few sites, or groups of sites, of which there are substantial upstanding remains.

The events which eventually prompted this development in England took place in the first half of the sixteenth century, in the time of Henry VIII. Very briefly, Henry, in his determination to divorce Catherine of Aragon, had broken with the Pope and, as a result, was faced in the years 1538–9 with the possibility of an invasion by both France and Spain. In the face of such a formidable threat some decisive action on coastal defences was needed. No amount of tinkering with existing castles would provide the answer and Henry's solution was a string of castles (although 'forts' might be a better designation), around the south-east corner of England, designed on principles quite different from those of traditional medieval castles and with the needs of artillery specifically in mind. Even so, in terms of design, Henry's castles were a short-lived type, being superseded within the same century by artillery fortifications based on the angle-bastion principle (below), which was then to hold the field for the next three centuries or so.

Among the most important of Henry's castles were Deal, Walmer and Sandown, 'the three castles which keep the Downs'. The Downs is a stretch of water between the Kent coast and the Goodwin Sands which provides a safe anchorage and was an important, not to say key, position in the days of sail, particularly in times of war. It is not surprising, therefore, that Henry chose to build three castles along the three mile stretch of coast overlooking and commanding the Downs as part of his coastal defences in the invasion scare of 1538–9. Of the three Deal is the largest and best preserved (Pl. 97). Sandown has been largely eroded by the sea and Walmer, although substantially intact, has

97 Deal Castle, Kent.

been much added to by reason of its function as the official residence of the Lords Warden of the Cinque Ports.

The outermost feature at Deal is a stone-lined, dry moat *c.* 50 ft wide and 16 ft deep which in plan follows, although not precisely, the six-lobed shape of the main structure (Fig. 29). This rises in three stages, the first stage being the six-lobed portion just mentioned. These lobes are, in fact, six semi-circular bastions projecting from a circular building, although because the bastions occupy most of the circumference, the circular nature of the building is not very apparent. The flat roofs of these bastions were the platforms for the main, heavy armament of the castle. From a continuous gallery in the basement, lighter hand-held guns could sweep the moat from fifty-three gun-ports, should an enemy penetrate that far. Above and within the main bastions rose the central structure or keep of the castle, a round tower with six inner, semi-circular bastions attached at a slightly lower level. Hand-gun ports in the walls of these inner bastions could command the outer areas if need be, while other heavier guns could be mounted on their flat roof and on the flat roof of the central tower. There were thus in all five tiers of guns, three heavy, roof-mounted tiers and two lighter, hand-held tiers, firing through gun-ports. The castle had a single entrance on the west side, via a stone-built causeway with (originally) a drawbridge at its inner end. The bastion facing due west formed the gatehouse, with a porter's lodge and an entrance hall. The back wall of the entrance hall housed a gun-port, enabling a cannon to be

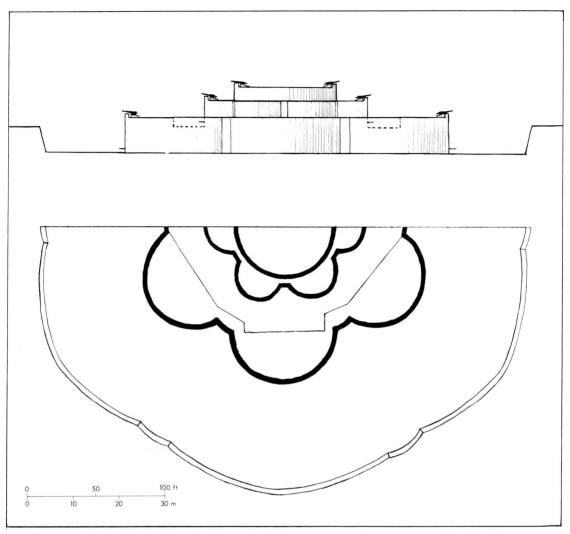

Fig. 29   Cross-section and half-plan of Deal Castle, Kent.

pointed directly at the gate in time of
danger.

Deal embodies the main ideas
underlying the design of Henry VIII's
castles. Walmer was the same sort of castle
on a smaller scale. Instead of the six main
bastions it had only four (a quatrefoil
plan), and it rose in only two stages
instead of three, the central feature being
a simple round tower with no attached
inner bastions as at Deal. It was
surrounded by a dry moat (of quatrefoil
plan), crossed by a causeway leading to a

gatehouse in one of the bastions, in plan
virtually a duplicate of Deal. Sandown
Castle, the third of the Downs forts, was
very similar to Walmer, with four semi-
circular bastions surrounding a circular
tower or keep, although very little now
remains to be seen on the ground.

The three Downs castles quite clearly
form a group linked by a common plan.
The remainder of Henry's castles,
although conforming to the same
principles, display a little more variety in
their layout. Sandgate and Camber, a

little further around the Kent coast beyond Dover, both have a central circular, keep-like tower, as in the three castles already considered. At Camber this tower stands at the centre of a twelve-sided outer defence, with D-shaped bastions, symmetrically placed, occupying four of the sides. At Sandgate, now partly destroyed, there are two lines beyond the central tower and the overall plan is triangular with outward curving sides and rounded corners.

Apart from the castles along the Kent coast, Henry either built from new, or adapted from existing structures, a whole series of artillery fortifications at various vulnerable points along the south coast. Two of the best preserved of these are at St Mawes and Pendennis in Cornwall, on opposite sides of the Fal estuary. St Mawes has a central circular tower surrounded by three roughly semi-circular bastions forming a generally triangular plan (Pl. 99). Pendennis is circular in plan with the main gun platform concentric with the central tower. Late in the sixteenth century Henry's original fort at Pendennis was enclosed within a much larger fortification, rectangular in plan and equipped with angle bastions in the fashion which was to become the standard for the next two or three centuries (Pl. 100). Among other fortifications built or adapted by Henry (in various states of survival), are Netley Castle, Calshot Castle and Hurst Castle in the Southampton/Solent area, Dartmouth and Kingswear, defending the Dart estuary in Devon, and Portland and Sandsfoot castles, defending Portland harbour in Dorset.

98   Deal Castle: the gatehouse.

99 St Mawes Castle, Cornwall.

100 Pendennis Castle, Cornwall.

One of Henry's castles, Southsea, just east of Portsmouth, is quite different from the others with their rounded bastions and circular central towers. Its central feature is, in fact, a rectangular tower or keep (*c.* 60 ft square), rising above the main structure which is distinctly angular in plan. It consists of a long rectangle, *c.* 240 × 80 ft with the ends forming two rectangular gun platforms and the keep occupying the central section. Two large triangular salients or bastions in the middle of the long north and south sides respectively give Southsea its unusual angular appearance and are a foretaste of the angle-bastion type of fortification which was to follow.

The Elizabethan addition to Pendennis Castle has been mentioned already, but the outstanding fortifications of the Elizabethan period are the walls of Berwick-on-Tweed (Northumb.), which embody the new ideas of artillery fortification developed in Italy during the previous half century (Pl. 101). The main structural features of the new style were angle bastions, massive triangular projections placed at the corners of, or midway along the walls of, fortifications so that from guns mounted on them, cross-fire could be directed against attackers to the front and flanking fire against attackers making a direct assault on the walls. These features are well exemplified at Berwick-on-Tweed, probably the best preserved artillery fortifications in the British Isles.

The existing fortifications, however, are

101 A flanker, the town walls, Berwick-on-Tweed.

102   Artillery embrasures, Norham Castle, Northumberland.

by no means the earliest around the city. There are still remains of earthwork defences of the time of Edward I (1272–1307), and of the stone walls and towers added in the following centuries. Under Henry VIII attempts were made to adapt the medieval defences for artillery and under Edward VI (1547–53) an entirely new fortification was begun embodying the new principles of artillery defence. This was rectangular in plan (c. 400 × 350 ft) with great triangular bastions at each corner, projecting like arrowheads beyond the main walls. This structure was still unfinished in 1557 when it was decided to remodel the whole of the town defences to replace the still unsatisfactory medieval defences which Henry VIII had attempted to adapt to the needs of artillery warfare.

The new defences, begun in 1558 and designed by Sir Richard Lee, covered the northern and eastern (landward) sides of the town; the southern and western sides were defined by the River Tweed where riverside defences were intended but never completed. The new perimeter was smaller than the earlier medieval circuit, leaving about one-third of the walled town outside the new northern defences. The main features of the new system were five great angular bastions, at the north-western, north-eastern and south-eastern angles, and midway along the northern and eastern sides, with straight stretches of walling between. These straight sections consisted of an outer stone wall 10–12 ft thick, with internal buttresses every 15 ft or so, backed up by a great bank of earth, c. 90 ft wide, and it was the thickness of this backing which was intended to absorb the shock of artillery attack. The bastions

182

were built in the same way with the whole triangular internal space filled with earth, except for access tunnels to the flankers. These were recesses between the bastions and the main walls from which fire could be directed along the walls against attackers attempting to scale or undermine them (Pl. 101). The Berwick fortifications are important for two reasons; first, simply because they have survived when so much else in the field of artillery defence has been destroyed; and second, because they belong to the early period of bastion-type artillery fortifications and are, therefore, important not only in the context of British military engineering but also in that of mainland Europe as well.

Equally well preserved, although considerably later in date, is Fort George near Inverness, on which work began *c.* 1747, that is, nearly two centuries after the Berwick fortifications. Although there are changes in the details, Fort George is substantially the same type of fortification as Berwick. It is built on a promontory site and at either end of the rampart on the landward side are great diamond-shaped bastions providing firing positions both to the front and to the side, along the face of the main rampart (Pl. 103). The recessed flankers of Berwick which gave the bastions their arrowhead shape have now gone. The bastions at the middle of the two long sides have likewise lost their recessed flankers; otherwise they too are of very much the size and shape of those at

103   Fort George, Inverness, Highland

Berwick. At the outer end of the promontory where the fort narrows there is a single composite bastion, somewhere between a full angle bastion and the adjacent mid-rampart type. Beyond the main fort on the landward side there is a wide ditch across the promontory, crossed by a bridge, with a 'ravelin' or fortified outwork beyond, supporting a central triangular bastion and two flanking subsidiary bastions commanding the direct approach to the fort.

The last group of fortifications to be considered in this survey of the British Isles are the martello towers of the nineteenth century which are, in a sense, a return to a basic type represented in virtually all periods: the broch tower of the prehistoric period; the various towers of the Roman period; the rectangular, polygonal and round tower-keeps of the medieval period; and the tower-houses of northern England, Scotland and Ireland. In all of these the tower form (i.e. accommodation, for whatever purpose, stacked up vertically) is presumably deemed to provide the best method of defence in the particular conditions obtaining at the time.

The term 'martello' is derived from Mortella Point in Corsica where in 1794 an ancient watch tower, one of a number in the area, proved so resistant to artillery bombardment that the British army and naval officers involved in the attack were convinced that this was an outstanding type of fortification. When, after the resumption of hostilities against Napoleon in 1803, the question of defence became a matter of urgency, one of the proposals was for a line of 'martello towers', as they were now called, along the southern and eastern coasts in the areas where an invading army might be expected to land. In spite of the urgency it was some two years after the first proposal before work actually got under way, in 1805. In fact, by then the immediate threat was over. In the same year Napoleon abandoned the idea of invading England and turned his 'Army of England' against Austria. Nevertheless, work proceeded although it was not until 1808 that the south coast system was finished. It then consisted of seventy-three towers along the 50 mile stretch of the Sussex and Kent coast, from Eastbourne (Pl. 105) to Folkestone. Later, a seventy-

104 Fort George, the barracks.

105   Martello tower, Eastbourne.

fourth tower was added to the western end
of the system, at Seaford, in Sussex. These
were all straightforward martello towers
mounting a single gun. Associated with
them were two larger towers or forts each
mounting eleven guns, obviously
something much more elaborate than the
martello towers. In the succeeding four
years, from 1808–12, the east coast system
was built, involving another twenty-nine
towers from Clacton in Essex to Aldeburgh
in Suffolk. By 1812 the whole system was
complete. One hundred and three
martello towers, together with more
conventional fortifications, covered the
most vulnerable parts of the south and
east coast. In fact, in spite of their
formidable appearance, they were never
put to the test. The invasion never came
and their guns never fired against an
enemy.

The external appearance of a martello
tower is that of an inverted flower or plant
pot, with a pronounced inward batter or
slope to the walls (Fig. 30). They are
about 33 ft high, with two storeys, and
between 48 and 55 ft in diameter at the
base. They are, in fact, oval rather than
truly circular and so positioned that they
present their narrower elevation to the sea.
The internal space is placed towards the
landward end of the oval, leaving the
greatest possible thickness of wall (*c.* 13 ft)
to the sea front. From this thickness the
wall gradually tapered to about 5 ft on the
landward side. The towers were built of
brick rendered with stucco and appear to
have been very strong in terms of
building. The bricks were bonded with a
mixture of lime, ash and hot tallow which
sets to a rock-like consistency, and
martello towers have proved difficult to
adapt or destroy, at least by human
agency. Some towers were surrounded by
ditches and some were not. There seems to
have been no consistency about this and

Fig. 30   Outline plan and section of a martello tower.

obviously it was not something which was rigidly laid down as part of the martello formula. The single entrance doorway was at first floor level, there being no entrance, nor indeed any windows or other opening, at ground floor level.

Internally the arrangements were fairly simple. The circular space available for accommodation etc. (*c*. 30 ft in diameter) had a round pillar at the centre, from basement to vaulted roof. Radial walls from this pillar divided the space into a number of smaller rooms. At first floor level these were for the accommodation of the garrison. In most cases the entrance, which was at this level, led into a small lobby from which opened three other rooms, the largest of which was for the men of the garrison, up to twenty-four in number. There was a single window, a fireplace and, in the thickness of the wall, a staircase to the gun platform above. There was a smaller room for the officer in charge, likewise equipped with a single

window and a fireplace, and the third room was a quartermaster's store. The vaulted ceiling of the first floor supported a roof up to 10 ft thick not only to support the heavy armament above but also to provide the same sort of protection from attack as the surrounding walls. The ground floor was reached by a trap-door and ladder and was used for the storage, not only of ammunition but also of considerable supplies of food and water, since the towers were intended to be capable of withstanding a long siege. The armament on the roof was usually a single (24-pounder) gun, which could pivot through 360 degrees, although some of the east coast forts had additional smaller guns as well.

Of the original 103 martello towers only 43 survive, some of them in ruinous condition. However, moves are now being made to restore a number of them to their original state. One of the south coast towers, No. 24 at Dymchurch in Kent, was restored by the then Ministry of Public Buildings and Works (now the Department of the Environment) in 1966 and is now open to the public during the summer months. Several others are under restoration at the present time.

*　　*　　*

As far as the present work is concerned martello towers mark the end of some two and a half thousand years of fortification, from c. 800 BC to c. AD 1800. During this long span of time there were few, if any, periods when some sort of protection was not required, either by the population at large against outside enemies, or by local communities against aggressive neighbours. Although inevitably the circumstances and the peoples involved changed considerably during these centuries, it is a noticeable fact that the solutions adopted were often very similar. The tower, for example, in the form of the broch, appears early in the story, and thereafter reappears again and again in most of the subsequent periods, albeit in varying forms: Roman signal towers, medieval keeps, post-medieval tower-houses, martello towers. Although the purposes which these towers were designed to serve were different, nevertheless the tower form (i.e. the use of elevation as a safety device) represents a solution common to all. Towers are one of the important basic elements in the story of fortification in the British Isles, and indeed in most others areas as well.

The second type of solution to the problem of defence was provided by the enclosing curtain wall, which lacked the advantages of elevation but which protected a much larger area of ground, larger than any tower could ever embrace. The curtain wall principle is exemplified in prehistoric hillforts, in Roman forts and camps, and in Roman and medieval town walls. Whereas the accommodation offered by a tower was necessarily limited, that offered by an enclosing curtain wall was extremely flexible and could be designed to contain and protect very large communities, including whole cities. whole cities.

In fact, the answer to most defence problems seems to have been a combination of the two basic features just described, the balance of the combination varying from period to period. Although the tower occasionally stood alone (the broch tower, for example), more often than not it stood within some sort of curtain wall which acted as an additional, outer line of defence. Equally, although the curtain wall was sometimes the only form of defence (in Iron Age hillforts, for example), more often than not it was supplemented by towers and turrets which added to its effectiveness. In the medieval period combinations of towers and curtain walls, often of many different periods, produced castles of great complexity and strength which are landmarks in the history of fortification.

The monuments of yesterday have always been documents worthy of study. In a rapidly changing era, with different values, this is more than ever true. And if such documents are worthy of study then they are surely worthy of preservation, for what they are and what they represent. Any civilization which neglects its future will certainly come to regret it one day, if only for economic reasons. But for a civilization which neglects its past the regrets will be much more profound and long lasting. In Britain at least, although much has been lost, much more of our priceless heritage is still preserved: and it is priceless, for no amount of money can ever replace it. For us there is still time to ensure that it continues to be preserved, for the pleasure and instruction of generations still to come.

Bibliography

Brown, R. A., *English Castles*, London, 1976.

Bruce, J. C., *Handbook to the Roman Wall* (12th ed.), Newcastle-upon-Tyne, 1966.

Collingwood, R. G. and Richmond, I. A., *The Archaeology of Roman Britain*, London, 1969, Chapters III, IV, & V.

Cruden, S., *The Scottish Castle*, London, 1960.

Cunliffe, B. W., *Iron Age Communities in Britain*, London, 1974, Chapter 13 (Hillforts).

Divine, D., *The North-west Frontier of Rome*, London, 1969.

Evans, E. E., *Prehistoric and Early Christian Ireland*, London, 1966.

Feachem, R. W., 'The Hillforts of Northern Britain', in *The Iron Age in Northern Britain* (ed. A. L. F. Rivet), Edinburgh, 1966, Chapter 4.

Forde-Johnston, J., *Hillforts of the Iron Age in England and Wales*, Liverpool, 1976.

Forde-Johnston, J., *Prehistoric Britain and Ireland*, London, 1976, Chapters 8 & 9.

Gascoigne, B. & G., *Castles of Britain*, London, 1975.

Grinsell, L. V., *The Archaeology of Wessex*, London, 1958, Chapter 10 (Hillforts).

Hamilton, J. R. C., 'Brochs and Broch-builders', in *The Northern Isles* (ed. F. T. Wainwright), London, 1962, Chapter VI.

Hamilton, J. R. C., 'Forts, Brochs and Wheelhouses', in *The Iron Age in Northern Britain* (ed. A. L. F. Rivet), Edinburgh, 1966, Chapter 6.

Harding, D. W., *The Iron Age in Lowland Britain*, London, 1974, Chapter 4 (Fortifications and Warfare).

Hogg, A. H. A., *Hillforts of Britain*, London, 1975.

Hogg, G., *Castles of England*, Newton Abbot, 1970.

Leask, H. G., *Irish Castles and Castellated Houses*, Dundalk, 1951.

Nash-Williams, V. E., *The Roman Frontier in Wales*, Cardiff, 1954.

O'Riordain, S. P., *Antiquities of the Irish Countryside*, London, 1953 (Irish Forts).

Ramm, H. G. *et al.*, *Shielings and Bastles* (HMSO), London, 1970.

Renn, D. F., *Norman Castles in Britain*, London, 1968.

Saunders, A. D., *Deal and Walmer Castles* (HMSO), London, 1971.

Simpson, W. D., *Castles in England and Wales*, London, 1969.

Sorrell, A., *British Castles*, London, 1973.

Sutcliffe, S., *Martello Towers*, Newton Abbot, 1972.

Thomas, N., *Guide to Prehistoric England*, London, 1960.

Thompson, A. H., *Military Architecture in England during the Middle Ages*, London, 1912.

Toy, S., *The Castles of Great Britain*, London, 1953.

Tranter, N., *The Fortified House in Scotland* (5 vols), Edinburgh, 1970 (vol. 5).

Turner, H. L., *Town Defences in England and Wales*, London, 1971.

Index